ATYP

INTERSECTION

CURRENCY PRESS
SYDNEY

ATYP
Australian Theatre
for Young People

CURRENCY PLAYS

First published in 2017
by Currency Press Pty Ltd,
PO Box 2287, Strawberry Hills, NSW, 2012, Australia
enquiries@currency.com.au
www.currency.com.au

Cataloguing-in-publication data for this title is available from the National Library of Australia website: www.nla.gov.au

Typeset by Emma Rose Smith for Currency Press.
Front cover shows Moreblessing Maturure.
Cover photograph: Luke Stambouliah.
Graphic design: Justin Stambouliah.

Currency Press acknowledges the Traditional Owners of the Country on which we live and work. We pay our respects to all Aboriginal and Torres Strait Islander Elders, past and present.

Contents

ATYP would like to acknowledge the support of the Graeme Wood Foundation, without whom this would not be possible. Thank you to Julie and John and all at the Bundanon Trust, the 2016 National Studio mentors: Mary Anne Butler, Angus Cerini and Sue Smith, and the Blue Room Theatre.

Thank you to all the writers from the 2016 National Studio who created such a beautiful environment in which to create new work: Angela Collins, Farnoush Parsiavashi, Thomas De Angelis, Brenden Snow, Eliza Oliver, Peter Beaglehole, Louis Klee, Zoe Ridgway, Michelle Sewell, Isabella Jacob, Suzannah Kennett Lister, Honor Webster-Mannison, Kevin Ngo, Laura Lethlean, Jordan Shea, Mark Tripodi, Lewis Treston, Anita Sanders, Isabelle McDonald, Jackson Used, and Charles O'Grady.

Introduction

Fraser Corfield

I'm sure it won't come as a surprise to learn that Australian Theatre for Young People (ATYP), the national youth theatre company, is committed to commissioning and developing plays that young people can perform. Our long-term vision is to create a body of work broad enough and specific enough to connect with every young Australian. At ATYP our work is not driven by a need to be educational, though we always support our productions with learning resources. We are looking to generate stories that hold an audience's attention because they are detailed, well drafted, unexpected and driven by an underlying truth.

We believe all the best theatre is written to be enjoyed, both in the telling and the watching. At times confronting, surprising, hilarious or deeply uncomfortable, these are stories that reflect the experiences of growing up and growing older. For that reason much of our work comes with a language or content warning. Like life, not all the themes and language are well behaved.

Intersection is a collection of short stories for the stage written by some of Australia's leading young playwrights. Each year a collection of writers aged between 18 and 26 attend the National Studio, a week-long playwriting retreat lead by some of the nation's leading playwrights and dramaturges. During the week, the group map out a place, event, item or theme that could link a range of teenage characters. They then write seven-minute scenes for 17-year-old actors. ATYP selects ten of these pieces for production. Those pieces become *Intersection*—the meeting place between different teenage lives.

This publication is the first in what we expect to be an annual instalment of short works for the stage. Following in the footsteps of ATYP's hugely successful *Voices Project, Intersection* will build over coming years to offer young actors a range of short plays with characters and situations that they can understand and relate to. Because that is the fundamental principle behind all good acting. When a character speaks in a speech rhythm that you know in your bones, dealing with issues that you see around you every day, in an environment not unlike the one you live in, then you can portray that character with the depth and detail it deserves.

I hope you will come on the *Intersection* journey with us. Feel free to pick and choose between the pieces you read in this publication and those in coming years. Their purpose is to instil an excitement and love of theatre and the storytelling process. If you would like to discuss *Intersection* or any of our other plays further, don't hesitate to contact us.

Fraser Corfield is Artistic Director of ATYP.

Director's Note

Katrina Douglas

My *Intersection* journey began one night in the beautiful Arthur and Yvonne Boyd Education Centre at Bundanon Trust. I was a bit frazzled from the drive down from Sydney and was feeling a tad concerned about the task that lay ahead. Directing one new play is a massive challenge, let alone ten short scenes by early-career playwrights. How was I going to turn ten disparate stories into one coherent performance? What if the writing was under-developed and inconsistent? What had I signed up for?

It took all of about one minute for my concerns to evaporate. For over three hours I listened in awe as the writers read their scenes. Characters leapt off the page, worlds unfolded and scenes took surprising turns. The writing was fresh, provocative and insightful. This wasn't work written by young writers. This was work written by writers. Writers with important stories to tell us if we choose to listen.

The eleven scenes in this collection show the complexities, tensions and joy of growing up today. They reveal the secret lives of young people at turning points in their lives. The characters and stories are inherently contemporary but they speak to a moment in time that everyone will recognise and relate too. It's been a privilege to bring them to life with 27 fantastic artists.

Here is the future of Australian theatre. As you'll see, that future is going to be extremely exciting.

Katrina Douglas is a director and producer with a passion for creating new work in collaboration with artists and communities.

Top: Last night of the National Studio 2016, Bundanon.

Left: First day of rehearsals, Walsh Bay.

Intersection was first produced by the Australian Theatre for Young People at Studio 1, The Wharf, Sydney, on 1 February 2017, with the following cast:

Little Differences	
CLAUDIA	Rebecca Gulia
DOM	Elliot Falzon
The Track and the Church	
PARKER	Jackson Williams
JOSHY	Hudson Musty
Yield	
CHARLIE	Alex Chalwell
WILL	Darius Williams
Pray 4 Mojo	
ACHILLES	Adam Stepfner
PATROCLUS	Kurt Pimblett
Blueberry Girl Grows Up	
BLUEBERRY GIRL	Esther Randles
The Arcade	
KAROLINA	Ingrid Leighton
STUART	Steffan Lazarevic
Dive	
JERRY	Iris Simpson
BILL	Alex Chorley
Palaces of Montezuma	
NADINE	Sonia Elliott
HARPER	Tamara Bailey
HASSAN	Ilai Swindells
Cassie and Saoirse	
CASSIE	Monica Kumar
SAOIRSE	Asha Boswarva
Bottlefeeders	
SARAH	May Tran

Director, Katrina Douglas
Assistant Director, Phoebe Adler-Ryan
Dramaturge, Jennifer Medway
Sound Designer, Tom Hogan
Set, Props and Costume Designer, Isabel Hudson
Lighting Designer, Emma Lockhart-Wilson
Stage Manager, Ruth Hollows
Production Manager, Lauren Makin

We encourage anyone producing and casting this work to consider performers from diverse backgrounds.

A name without dialogue next to it (i.e., LENA:), indicates a silence in which a character choses not to speak or is unable to speak.

A slash (/) indicates a point of overlap. If at the start of a line, it means the next line is spoken simultaneously.

A dash (—) indicates a point of interruption.

Little Differences

Jordan Shea

A playground. DOM *is listening to 'Uptown Funk' full blast. He's dancing. And I mean dancing.* CLAUDIA *enters.*

CLAUDIA: Hey!

> DOM *continues to dance. Ignoring her.*

Oi!

> CLAUDIA *goes over to* DOM, *rips his headphones out of his ears.*

DOM: What the fuck!?

CLAUDIA: You listening to some extremist bullshit or something?

DOM: What the fuck did you say?

CLAUDIA: Calm down dickhead.

DOM: You come here to hang out or what?

CLAUDIA: You need to come to class.

DOM: It's geography. I don't need it. I know where things are. It's only if someone comes up to me, puts a gun to my head and asks me for the longitude and latitude of a country, I'm fucked.

> *Pause.*

I used to do this all the time anyway. At my old school.

CLAUDIA: Before you got kicked out?

DOM: We moved. Wasn't my choice. We moved. I didn't get kicked out. Who the fu—

CLAUDIA: Why you gotta be so aggro? You fuckin' shrug people off like that, people don't want anything to do with you. Any of you, and—

DOM: Any of us?

CLAUDIA: You know what I mean. Drop your act, thinking you're fucking king shit—

DOM: Aren't you meant to be my buddy?

CLAUDIA: It's not a big deal if I quit. Someone else can do it.

DOM: They chose you. For a reason.

CLAUDIA: Because I've been a shit lately. A lot. Then they give me something to do. I don't fucking get it. I sent out a couple of text messages to some bitch. She started it though. Got this rumour going that I slept with her boyfriend. She got a couple of after school detentions, I got stuck with you.

DOM: You think I started those fights don't you?

CLAUDIA: Not what I said. But you being angry doesn't really make a good name for yourself does it?

DOM: Nah, nor for all those idiots that started punching on the beach hey? Because I'm mates with them. Cousins, or whatever it is you think.

CLAUDIA *goes to exit.*

I know your brother started one of the fights.

CLAUDIA: He was off his face. His mates made him do it, and they got carried away. He didn't start shit. Don't say that. You should probably be a bit smarter instead of running your mouth like that. What were you doing when it was all happening?

DOM: Helping my dad.

CLAUDIA: Oh yeah, doing what?

DOM: He thought it was a good idea to sell kebabs at the carpark. You know the one up near the sand dunes?

CLAUDIA: I know the one.

DOM: His idea of peacekeeping. Better than what the pigs did.

CLAUDIA: They were doing a lot more than you guys.

DOM: Nothing better than some halal meat pre riot hey?

Pause.

I'm not that bad.

CLAUDIA: Who told you about Joel starting the fights?

DOM: I heard.

CLAUDIA: You've been here a day. Have you just been stalking me? Googling me or some shit? Trying to find out stuff? They watch your internet use here so just be careful what you're looking for. Don't want people thinking you're gonna do something stupid.

DOM: My cousin told me about your brother.

CLAUDIA: Oh, no shit.

DOM: Yeah. He went down to the beach that day too.

CLAUDIA: Which one was he? I mean they were pretty outnumbered.

DOM: You think that's funny? About a thousand to one. He was fucking terrified. He wasn't even there to protest, he was going to get more onions for our kebab stand.

CLAUDIA: He probably shouldn't have been walking there. I mean, he should've seen what was going on. Or you should've just brought more onions.

DOM: What, because a couple of idiots were hanging out looking for someone to kick the shit out of?

CLAUDIA: He get hurt?

DOM: Cops fished him out before they could really do some damage. Just got yelled at. By people like you. But hey, that's most of us.

CLAUDIA: I get beeped at. Cat-called. Stupid shit gets said to me *all* the fucking time. Heaps. By people like you.

DOM: I've never done that shit.

CLAUDIA: Could've been you this morning. In your hotted up car and—

DOM: Nah.

Pause.

CLAUDIA: Why'd you leave your last school?

DOM: Parents moved. Mum works in nursing. We just go where she goes.

CLAUDIA: So nothing to do with tagging?

DOM: Tagging? Who told you that?

CLAUDIA: I heard things.

DOM: What the fuck did you hear?

CLAUDIA: I got to listen into a staff meeting when they brought me into be your buddy.

DOM: Fuck yeah … What? They talk about me?

CLAUDIA: Yeah sure did … Afif.

DOM: Where'd you get that from? Who told you—

CLAUDIA: It's your name.

DOM: Nah, it's Dom. Dominic. Patron saint of stars.

CLAUDIA: That's a bit gay.

DOM: No-one fuckin' calls me Afif except my cousins. Afif is just a name. Just a boring name.

CLAUDIA: Where's it from?

DOM: How the fuck should I know? Where does Claudia come from?

CLAUDIA: Grandma's name. Well, it's my Pop's name—Claude. But I ended up being a girl so I got Claudia.

DOM: Claude sounds French. You French? French is hot.

CLAUDIA: No, we're Aussie. I just got Claudia because…well, I dunno why I got Claudia.

Pause.

Can I call you Afif?

DOM: Get fucked.

CLAUDIA: Afif is sort of sexy.

Pause.

DOM: You don't think the patron saint of stars is sexy?

CLAUDIA: Depends on what Afif means.

DOM: Modest. I don't even know what that means. So I stick to Dom. So should you.

CLAUDIA: What about 'Fif'?

DOM: What about get fucked?

CLAUDIA *nods.*

CLAUDIA: If you don't come with me, I'll just go out to the bins for a smoke and say I was looking all over the place for you.

DOM: You'd do that?

CLAUDIA: I fucking hate geography.

DOM: Yeah cool.

Pause.

You could stay here for a smoke.

CLAUDIA: Yeah, sure. You got any?

DOM: Nah, I was gonna ask you.

CLAUDIA: I usually steal some from my brother. But Dad's checking his room all the time so he's useless.

DOM: Fair. Your dad checking his room for any of that like white only bullshit, knives and stuff?

CLAUDIA: Does your dad check your room for bombs and stuff or—

DOM: What the fuck does that mean?

CLAUDIA: Shut up.

Pause.

DOM: Just hang out here for a bit. If you want, I mean, you don't have to. You can if you like.

CLAUDIA: You gonna play that stupid music too loud or what?

DOM: What's wrong with uptown funk?

CLAUDIA: Old. Really old. You got lemonade on there?

DOM: Nah, I hate that shit. Need something with a good rhythm.

CLAUDIA: You a DJ now?

DOM: I dropped a few beats at my Year Ten formal. People still talk about it. It was the biggest thing to happen at that school.

CLAUDIA: What, like a legacy?

DOM: Yeah. They called me DJ Halal.

CLAUDIA: Nice. You should do it for our formal.

DOM: That's soon hey?

CLAUDIA: Yeah in a couple of months. I don't like it the whole formal thing. Afters is sick. We're doing it at my place.

Pause.

You coming?

DOM: Yeah, I guess. I mean I don't have plans.

CLAUDIA: Come to afters then.

Pause.

DOM: Your friends would fuckin' hate me.

CLAUDIA: Why do you think that?

DOM: They look like your brothers. All of them. They'd either not talk to me or just be total fuckwits. I've seen what they're like in packs. It's like they've got something to prove.

CLAUDIA: Yeah? Would I fit in at one of your parties then?

DOM: If you wanna come out away from here, sure. Who the fuck do I hang out with around here? No-one else looks like me. I can't really be the token guy. Because being token is usually kinda cool. People love the token guy. Token Asian, token black guy.

CLAUDIA: You miss your old school.

DOM: No shit.

CLAUDIA: You're overthinking this whole thing. Stop fuckin' overreacting, pull your head in and think outside for a minute.

DOM: You don't know shit. It's easy for you, cos your friends are all around.

CLAUDIA: You're not making much of an effort. First period and you're out here listening to shit tunes.

DOM: You should go.

CLAUDIA: I already got a bad name, people aren't gonna worry if I turn up late or not turn up at all. I don't really care hey.

DOM: I just can't stand the way they look at me when I walk in. I mean, what the fuck was that, the principal introducing me to the whole school on the first day?!

CLAUDIA: He does that with everyone. It's just a first day thing.

DOM: People look at me like I'm some kind of terrorist. Like I'm gonna blow the whole place up, you know, 'boom!'

CLAUDIA: … Are you?

DOM: Are you stupid?

CLAUDIA: I'm kidding.

DOM: Don't say that shit. I'm just playing it up.

CLAUDIA: No shit.

> *Pause.*

DOM: I might come to formal. I mean the afters.

CLAUDIA: Oh yeah? Just the afters? Fuck it just turn up to the whole thing. The formal I mean.

DOM: Nah. I got no-one to go with.

> *Pause.*

Which is cool! You know that's cool, I don't really want to go. But afters sounds alright. Your brother will be there yeah? I don't want him to try anything because, you know, if he does, I'll be ready.

> DOM *arcs up to himself.* CLAUDIA *laughs.*

CLAUDIA: You're a fuckwit. You're like him. Thinking ahead, thinking who's gonna be around you, near you, all that. Fuck. You see why those riots started yeah? Because of idiots like you.

DOM: Wasn't me. And—

CLAUDIA: I said idiots *like* you.

DOM: Yeah, sure.

CLAUDIA: Joel might not even be at afters. He'll probably just be at the beach getting stoned.

DOM: Yeah good.

DOM *continues to arc himself up.*

Your friends going to your afters too?

CLAUDIA: Yeah

DOM: Yeah cool, they're hot.

CLAUDIA: If you had friends I'd probably think they're alright.

DOM: Awwww, get fucked! I'm pretty hot.

CLAUDIA: You're fuckin rough.

Pause.

Which is alright.

DOM: Yeah, good. I mean I've seen your friends, they all look the same. Especially in a group they just kinda blend into one. One big blonde, tartan, white group. Hairspray smell. Like, I can't understand a word you're saying.

CLAUDIA: I can hear your crew from ages away.

DOM: I don't have a crew.

CLAUDIA: You know what I mean. Everything is just like: 'Aw yeah, fuck, fuck, fuck. Yeah bro, sick bro. Aw fuck bro'. Like you're in competition with each other. All finding out who's the biggest dickhead.

DOM: Do you like those girls?

CLAUDIA: Nah they're bitches.

DOM *laughs.*

I just have to hang out with them. Just a given. I don't really have a choice.

DOM: What, so, if people saw you and me hanging out—

CLAUDIA: Outside of school? Yeah it'd be weird. People would probably be a little shocked.

DOM: Right. I don't use enough hairspray or anything?

CLAUDIA: You could use a bit more actually. If you come to the formal—

DOM: Not going to the formal. Nah. I tell you what though, at the afters, I'll come in a full sheikh' get up. Full robes and everything. That'll shock them big time.

CLAUDIA: Just come to the formal.

DOM: Ha. Who with?

CLAUDIA: Me.

Pause.

DOM: Get fucked.

CLAUDIA: Why not? I don't care.

DOM: Your friends would think that is whacked. I mean seriously, they would think that is just out of this world.

CLAUDIA: Because I'm not taking someone who looks like my brother?

Pause.

You'll have to leave your prayer gear at home and dress normal though if you want to come to formal.

DOM: Oh, oh yeah of course. I mean I don't have any of that stuff anyway. I mean, if you wanna hang out with me, I'll have to check if you have any Southern Cross tats.

DOM *awkwardly laughs.*

CLAUDIA: I don't.

DOM: Yeah cool. You'd look good though, with one.

CLAUDIA: I fucking hate them. Joel and his mates got them, and a guy I used to hook up with had a few different ones. They're gross and weird.

DOM: Yeah I think so too. My cousin got something done in Arabic right across his back. In English it just says; 'I am me'. Like what the fuck does that mean?!

CLAUDIA: It looks good in Arabic though right.

DOM: Oh yeah beautiful, but we give him heaps of shit for it.

CLAUDIA: Same as Joel with his Southern Cross.

Pause.

DOM: You reckon people will say stuff if we turn up together?

CLAUDIA: Not to our faces. Just online, group chat, snap chat. But what's that gonna do right? I mean who actually gives a fuck.

DOM: I thought you would.

Did the teachers ask you to ask me?

CLAUDIA: Nah.

Pause.

You seem alright.

The Track and the Church

Zoe Ridgway

The action takes place at the BMX track. It exists offstage, where the audience is situated. PARKER *is sitting on the edge of the stage, legs hanging over the edge. He is in his school uniform, the tie loosened down from his collar.*

JOSHY *enters from the back of the stage, wheeling his clicking bike beside him. He is wearing a T-shirt, shorts and a backpack with a school tie hanging out of it. He walks up to* PARKER, *dropping his bike next to him.*

PARKER: Finally!

JOSHY: Thought Mr Bond would never get off my trail.

PARKER: Old mate Bondy.

JOSHY: The lunch duty queen.

PARKER: Nothing gets past him.

JOSHY: 'Cept for me. Led 'im past the stairs where that year twelve couple always suck each other's faces off.

PARKER: Diversion, nice.

JOSHY: Told ya I didn't need to pull a sickie. Why you in uniform?

PARKER: I had to wear it, for going through town, looks too suss otherwise.

JOSHY: It looks more suss I reckon.

PARKER: Nah dude, if you got your uniform on, you have a purpose.

JOSHY: Huh?

PARKER: In uniform, people assume you gotta note and you're meeting your mum at the chemist to pick up some antibiotics, can't have whooping cough going round school.

> JOSHY *taps his nose.*

JOSHY: But what if someone from school sees ya?

PARKER: Well, they are all at school aren't they?

> *Beat.*

JOSHY: Ah, gotcha.

> *Beat.*

[*Gesturing to his bike*] Best outta three?

PARKER: Maybe later.

JOSHY: Parker!

PARKER: What?

JOSHY: [*gesturing to the track*] The track is empty! Right now, all the juniors are sitting through assembly. We can be *the first of the day* to tear it up.

PARKER: I guess that's cool.

JOSHY: You guess!?

PARKER: Yeah.

JOSHY: It hasn't rained for weeks. The hills are nice, real dry, just asking for a good tearing.

PARKER: I don't know, I'm not in the mood for tearing.

JOSHY: But it's ya birthday!

PARKER: Maybe later.

> *Pause.*

JOSHY: Well, if ya don't wanna race, I better give ya your present.

PARKER: Present?

> *Beat.* JOSHY *fishes around in his pockets. Pulls out a newly rolled, slightly squashed joint.*

JOSHY: Here ya go birthday boy.

PARKER: Joshy! You wrapped it 'n all.

> PARKER *inspects the joint.*

… is this guy green?

> JOSHY *grins.*

You sly fuck.

JOSHY: Green for go.

> JOSHY *pulls a lighter out of his bag. He passes it to* PARKER.

Go on, open ya present Parker.

> PARKER *lights up, takes a drag and passes it to* JOSHY, *who in turn takes a drag. They pass it around for the remainder of the scene. There's a comfortable silence.*

PARKER: Seventeen.
JOSHY: Yep.

> *Beat.*

PARKER: It doesn't feel like it, you know?
JOSHY: Never does on the day.
PARKER: It used to.

> *Beat.*

Getting older used to be exciting. The presents, attention, cake, even just waking up in the morning. I mean, shit, if I was turning fourteen and a ladybug pissed on me it would be a sign from the Birthday Gods or some shit. The whole day was just wrapped up like a neat little parcel from my Aunty Pam.
JOSHY: [*to no-one in particular*] Those were happy birthdays.
PARKER: And eighteen's only just round the corner.
JOSHY: Fuck me.

> *Beat.*

PARKER: I feel so old.
JOSHY: Next year we'll vote, we'll drink, legally.
PARKER: Not in the States.
JOSHY: Man, let's not even go near twenty-one.

> *Beat.*

> PARKER *gets up as he speaks, walking around* JOSHY.

PARKER: It's just surreal.
JOSHY: Sur-real.
PARKER: People always ask if you feel older on the day.
JOSHY: I always get that man! Every fucking year!
PARKER: I mean …

> PARKER *takes a drag. Coughs.*

What is it like? To *feel* older …
JOSHY: Did we ever feel older?

> *Beat.*

PARKER: Well, maybe it wasn't feeling older, maybe it was feeling like …

JOSHY: [*to himself*] Feel-ing older.

PARKER: It felt like we earnt something.

JOSHY: Yeah!

PARKER: It's weird ...

JOSHY: It is weird!

PARKER: I mean getting older's guaranteed, y'know?

JOSHY: Everyone gets birthdays.

PARKER: *Everyone* gets birthdays.

> *Silence.*

> Do you ...

> *Beat.*

JOSHY: Do you?

PARKER: Never mind.

JOSHY: What?

> *Beat.*

PARKER: Do you ever feel like we are, you know, getting too old for the track?

JOSHY: [*jolting up*] What?

> JOSHY *stands as they talk.*

PARKER: I know how it sounds.

JOSHY: Fucking crazy is how it sounds!

PARKER: I know but—

JOSHY: —Why do you think we came here on ya birthday?

PARKER: It's our—

JOSHY: —Our place! We earnt it. We've been coming here since year six, longer than any other group. We've earnt it!

PARKER: That's what I mean though.

JOSHY: What?

PARKER: We are the only ones left from our year!

JOSHY: Well that's why we earnt it.

PARKER: We are almost in year twelve and still sharing with year eights!

JOSHY: They answer to us.

PARKER: You kidding? They don't respect us, they don't even listen to us when we say their tyre's flat. There's a new generation that's taking this place to shit.

Beat.

There's nothing we can do about it.

JOSHY: We could—

PARKER: —It's inevitable Joshy. When we graduate, they'll still be there, running it to the ground.

Beat.

I mean, we could …

JOSHY: What?

PARKER: We could start going to The Church.

JOSHY: The Church?!

JOSHY *reaches for the joint in* PARKER'*s hand. He moves it out of* JOSHY*'s reach.*

PARKER: I mean it.

JOSHY: All this seventeen shit is messing with you!

PARKER: I don't mean the fucking Sunday service, you know, The Church? On Barker Street?

JOSHY: Oh, you mean the Church cafe.

PARKER: What else would I mean?

JOSHY: Why didn't you just say cafe—why do you want to go to the Church cafe?!

PARKER: For a coffee?

JOSHY: Huh?

PARKER: They make coffee out the front.

JOSHY: So you want takeaway here?

PARKER: Coffee on bikes?

JOSHY: Where else would we have coffee?

PARKER: At the cafe?

JOSHY: *The cafe!* Prams and dogs tied to chairs go to the cafe. What's to do there?

PARKER: You can do stuff at the cafe. People do stuff there.

JOSHY: What stuff?

Beat.

PARKER: We can chat. About stuff.

JOSHY: *Chat*?!

PARKER: Talk over coffee.

JOSHY: *Talk over coffee.*
PARKER: People do it all the time.
JOSHY: But we are talking right now.
PARKER: So?
JOSHY: So, we don't need to go to a cafe to *talk.*
PARKER: Sure we don't—
JOSHY: —That weeds' fucking with your brain. Coffee? *Chat?*
PARKER: Well sure we don't *need* to chat there—
JOSHY: —*Stop* saying chat.
PARKER: Talk—whatever. You go there for the vibe.
JOSHY: But what about here?
PARKER: Huh?
JOSHY: What about the vibe here?

> *Silence.* PARKER *moves to the bike, kneels down and starts turning the nearest pedal. The chain slowly clicks over.*

[*To himself*] Vibe?

> *Pause.*

PARKER: Girls go to cafes.
JOSHY: My fucking lord.
PARKER: They do.
JOSHY: Why didn't ya just say this was about girls?
PARKER: It's not all about girls.
JOSHY: Cafés. Coffee. You need a wank that's what ya need—
PARKER: —That is not what I need! Not what I mean.

> *Beat. Awkward.*

My sister goes to cafes with her friend, Sonia T.
JOSHY: Why should I care if Sonia T. orders a fucking piccolo?
PARKER: Huh?
JOSHY: Some almond milk, espresso, fucking double shot piccolo.
PARKER: You've been to cafes!

> JOSHY *sighs.*

JOSHY: *Mum* used to go to cafes with that gardening group. But now she makes me pick up their piccolos and flat whites during my driving lessons!

Beat.

PARKER: I've heard The Church does good coffee. Sonia told me they did good coffee.

JOSHY: You 'chat' to Sonia?

PARKER: She's my sister's best friend. I run into her down my hallway all the time.

JOSHY: Oh.

PARKER: Maybe … we could go for a coffee with them sometime?

Silence.

JOSHY: *Oh.*

PARKER: What?

JOSHY: You little shit …

PARKER: What?!

JOSHY: You're bribing me.

PARKER: I'm not bribing y—

JOSHY: —You're bribing me with Sonia!

PARKER: That's not what I—

JOSHY: —Cut the shit, you know I've liked her since year ten.

PARKER: You never told me.

JOSHY: You *know* you know.

PARKER: Joshy—

JOSHY: —There's no question about you knowing. No fucking question. No way am I getting a coffee with Sonia, I don't even talk to Sonia! Don't think I know how to deal wi—with Sonia myself?

PARKER: No Joshy—

JOSHY: —Coffee's weird, you're making it all weird. You manipulating me Parker—you're mani—manipulating your best friend, for a coffee. We don't need fucking coffee!

Silence.

PARKER: I'm sorry.

Beat.

I just thought we could do somethin' different.

JOSHY: Different doesn't mean better.

Beat.

This is all ours, Parker, our place. I mean we're not even eighteen and we own all of this. Nothing beats a place that's ours. Nothing can.

Long silence.

PARKER *runs his hands through the dirt. Stoned out of his mind.*

PARKER: Are you feeling the ground right now?

Pause. JOSHY *feels the ground.*

JOSHY: It's … grainy.

PARKER: Grainy! It's grainy!

Pause. They continue feeling the dirt.

I can feel every grain, like, like every single grain of dirt.

Beat.

And they keep—

PARKER *snickers.*

JOSHY: —What?

PARKER: They keep—keep getting caught on our … fingerprints!

PARKER *pisses himself.* JOSHY *stares at him, running his hands through the dirt.*

Yield

Thomas De Angelis

In a field of golden wheat lies a fallen, dead gum tree, half severed from its stump, but still connected in a splintered mess. Wheat stalks lie crushed and broken beneath the tree. A creek gurgles nearby.

CHARLIE, *a young boy, aged about seventeen, walks up to the tree and mounts the fallen trunk. He jumps and throws his weight down in an effort to snap the tree off completely. The tree holds together. He jumps again. Nothing.*

CHARLIE *begins to jump on the tree with abandon, grunting as he goes. The tree cracks and splinters further, but doesn't come away from its stump.* CHARLIE *stops, exhausted, and gets down. Panting hard, and with tears streaming down his face, he makes one last attempt to sever the tree from its stump, throwing his foot squarely into the trunk.*

The tree barely moves at all.

CHARLIE *sobs. Then calms himself. Then wipes his face. Then leans back against the tree, facing out towards to the creek.*

WILL, *a boy of about seventeen, walks into the field.*

WILL: Hey.

> CHARLIE *looks around and sees* WILL. CHARLIE *nods his head in greeting and turns back towards the creek.* WILL *looks at the tree.*

[*To* CHARLIE] C'mon.

> *Together,* CHARLIE *and* WILL *jump on the trunk of the tree a few times. They stop.*

Needs a saw.

CHARLIE: I thought it was more dead.

WILL: Or an axe.

CHARLIE: Well, it needs to come out.

WILL: You can see why it fell over.

WILL *points to the stump, indicating that the tree is dead.*

CHARLIE: It fell over because somebody pulled it over.

WILL: Why d'you want to break it?

CHARLIE: I want it gone. It's ruining the crop.

WILL: Crop's fucked anyway.

CHARLIE: No, it's not.

WILL: It's gonna rain today.

 CHARLIE *and* WILL *both look up towards the sky in silence.*

CHARLIE: Maybe.

WILL: Dad says it's gonna rain. That's why we got it all in yesterday. Said that it's the only time of the year when a farmer prays for it *not* to rain. [*He turns to look at* CHARLIE] Did ya hear that the Butchers' field bin was stolen?

 CHARLIE *shakes his head.*

They woke up on Saturday, went to start, and then their field bin was missin'.

CHARLIE: Have they found it?

WILL: Nah. They had to hire one of those machine ones.

CHARLIE: They're expensive, those things.

WILL: Kid at school reckons they're worth more than you make off the crop.

CHARLIE: They're not that expensive.

WILL: At your school back in Sydney, how many farmers' kids are there?

CHARLIE: Not that many.

WILL: What are they mostly?

CHARLIE: Lawyers' kids. Doctors' kids. Lot of accountants.

WILL: But *your* friends—they're farmers' kids, right?

CHARLIE: Some of them.

 After a moment, CHARLIE *kicks the tree again.*

WILL: You're not gonna break it like that.

CHARLIE: I'm gonna try.

WILL: Mum's gonna ask me what we ended up doin' together and I don't want to have to lie to her. We shouldn't be hangin' out here. Remember we used to go down to the dam and throw rocks? There was an island in the middle. I can *drive* us down now.

CHARLIE: I'd really like it if you could just—

WILL: —I'm already lyin' to her about Saturday night.

CHARLIE: What did you do on Saturday night?

WILL: Went into town with Rob and that. Went to the pub.

CHARLIE: Which pub?

WILL: Royal. The one next to the Starlight Plaza. There was this girl there. Remember Sophie Flannery? Went to Saint Ed's with us.

CHARLIE: Yeah, I remember her.

WILL: I got with her.

CHARLIE: At the Royal?

WILL: Yep.

CHARLIE: Is she hot?

WILL: She's alright.

CHARLIE: And you want to tell your mum about that?

WILL: Mum always said she wanted a daughter. She says her boys just make her older.

CHARLIE: She wants a daughter, not some girl you hooked up with.

WILL: Well, I want to tell her, but if I tell her I have to tell her that I was at the Royal.

CHARLIE: Don't tell her.

WILL: Nah, I won't.

Pause. He looks off towards his property.

Dad gave me the day off to come and see you. You know, he changes at harvest. He gets all red in the face, yells all the time. It's like he thinks he's losin' money and not makin' it the way he carries on. But he just makes it harder. Starts too late and then rushes to finish before it rains.

CHARLIE: So, what's he doing today?

WILL: Clean up.

CHARLIE: How old's your dad?

WILL: I don't know—fifty something.

CHARLIE: How old's Rob?

WILL: Thirty-four.

CHARLIE: So your dad was twenty when he had him?

WILL: Musta been.

CHARLIE: Is Rob married?

WILL: He's got a bird. I don't like her. She's a townie. Cries all the
fuckin' time. Says she misses Sydney. I don't get it.

CHARLIE: Haven't you ever been?

WILL: I went to the Easter Show last year. Hated it.

CHARLIE: Why?

WILL: So many wogs. It wasn't about the country at all. It was about
showbags and cars doin' tricks in the showground. It's shit.

> *Pause.*

CHARLIE: I sang at the Easter Show last year.

WILL: What?

CHARLIE: I sang with a choir. We sang the National Anthem before the
Woodchopping.

WILL: You did what?

CHARLIE: The Woodchop … never mind.

> *Pause.* CHARLIE *bends down and picks up a stalk of wheat.*

Wheat looks so soft when you're driving past it, hey? When mum
was driving me yesterday, the wheat we passed looked really soft.
Like a blonde girl's hair.

WILL: Yeah, but—you go running through wheat it'll cut you up.

CHARLIE: I used to be able to run through it, when I was younger—
because I was smaller.

> *Pause.*

WILL: What's your dad gonna do now? You guys gonna sell?

CHARLIE: Did you get sent over here to ask me that?

WILL: Mum said you needed some distraction.

CHARLIE: I don't.

> *Pause.*

WILL: Dad was talkin' about it. Said if it had happened a bit earlier we
coulda helped you get the crop in. He started talkin' about buyin'
the property off you. You should sell it to dad if you decide to sell.
Don't sell it to some Chinese bloke.

CHARLIE: We're not selling.

WILL: But still. A Chinese company bought Meagher's place.

CHARLIE: The Meaghers probably wanted to sell.

WILL: Yeah, but that's not fair. We don't have that kind of money.

CHARLIE: Your dad struggles with the land he's got anyway.

WILL: We'd probably bring in a manager. I need something for when I'm old enough.

CHARLIE: So, you're staying out here?

WILL: Yeah. I'm not goin' back to school next year.

> *Pause.*

CHARLIE: Maybe we will sell. I don't know.

> *Pause.*

WILL: It's hard for everybody, but.

> *Pause.*

If you need somebody to talk to …

> *Pause. And then very quietly:*

Your dad shouldn't have done what he did—

> CHARLIE *turns around and punches* WILL *squarely in the jaw.*

CHARLIE: Fuck off!

WILL: What the fuck was that for?

> CHARLIE *takes another wild swing at* WILL, *but* WILL *dodges it. Then* WILL *launches at* CHARLIE, *and they wrestle and wrangle each other into a stalemate on the ground.* WILL *is stronger than* CHARLIE.

I was just bein' nice—

> CHARLIE, *writhing under* WILL, *finally submits.* WILL *gets off him and they stand, facing off.*

CHARLIE: I know why you came here. You already told me twice.

WILL: Yeah, well, you need help. You can't just punch someone like that. It's not OK.

CHARLIE: You, Mum, the hundred other people that just want to stop by the house to see how Dad's doing—telling him to give it a rest—

you're all no fucking help! And I'd really appreciate it if you could all just fuck off.

CHARLIE: I don't care.

WILL: Maybe you've got the same fuckin' shit going on that your dad does.

CHARLIE: Shut the fuck up!

WILL: It's hard for everybody—but we can't all neck ourself. Least he coulda done woulda been to do it from a fuckin' tree that could hold him up there!

CHARLIE: You say one more thing about him again and I'll kill you, I swear.

WILL: You're a dickhead, you know that? My mouth really hurts.

CHARLIE: Deserved it.

WILL: Are we all 'sposed to let you be a dumb cunt while we all keep going? Do ya' think—

CHARLIE: —You want to buy it—go ahead! I don't want it.

WILL: Nah, I wasn't sayin' that.

CHARLIE: Yes, you were. You don't think I can run the land, do you?

WILL: Do you?

CHARLIE: I could work it out.

WILL: Can't even clear this tree!

CHARLIE: I will fucking clear this tree—if I have to get the Hilux and crash into it I'll fucking clear this fucking tree.

> *Pause.*

WILL: You don't have to clear it. It was nice when it was up. Not strong enough to swing off—but it looked cool from far way. I reckon you'll miss it.

> *Pause.*

That's what pisses people off about you. You think it's just you that's stuffed.

CHARLIE: What?

WILL: Rob's already runnin' our place. What about me? That's why I asked. I wanted to know …

CHARLIE: Fine. It's yours.

WILL: Nah, I can't take it now …

Pause.

Sorry.

Pause.

CHARLIE: I've got a girlfriend. Back in Sydney.

WILL: Is she hot?

CHARLIE: She's beautiful and smart and for some reason she likes me. But she doesn't know. About any of this. And tonight was our formal and I had to make up some shit excuse about grandma being sick. Because I knew that if I told her the truth she'd freak out and think I had to leave forever.

Pause.

I might have to stay here. I don't want to.

WILL: It's not that bad.

CHARLIE: None of my … none of my dreams are here.

WILL: Well, you don't even sleep here most of the time. How can you have dreams here if you don't sleep here?

After a moment, CHARLIE *laughs.* WILL *doesn't understand why it's funny.*

CHARLIE: [*referring to the tree*] Give us a hand.

Together, CHARLIE *and* WILL *lift the trunk of the tree and scrunch it back into its splintered stump. They step back. The tree stays upright.*

Pray 4 Mojo

Charles O'Grady

A dilapidated concrete space. Looks like it could once have been a carpark or garage, or a storage space of some kind, but hasn't been used in many years. Moss grows through cracks in the floor, vines climb what is left of the walls. Bits and pieces of rubble, concrete and metal sit in piles, the largest of these in the upstage left corner. There is a large hole in the concrete wall there, which becomes the point of entrance and exit. The space looks like somewhere the city forgot, an eerie urban Sublime. There are puddles of water and random bits of debris. The graffiti on the back wall reads 'PRAY 4 MOJO'. Close to the centre there is a haphazard scrap metal contraption. In a vaguely humanoid shape, this contraption is known as 'the machine', or Mojo. Mojo was built by ACHILLES.

ACHILLES *sits in the ruins, talking softly to his machine.* PATROCLUS *enters through the smashed-in wall. These characters have never seen each other before.*

PATROCLUS: Oh.

    ACHILLES *starts.*

ACHILLES: What?

PATROCLUS: I'm—

ACHILLES: Who are—?

PATROCLUS: —sorry, I'll just—

ACHILLES: —no you don't have to—

PATROCLUS: —leave you, sorry, no-one else is ever—

ACHILLES: —I'm usually the only one—

PATROCLUS: —in here.

ACHILLES: Yeah.

    A long, awkward, frightened pause.

You don't have to go. If you don't want. Free country. Just no-one else has ever been here.

PATROCLUS: Sorry, I would have made more noise—

ACHILLES: Except the cat.

PATROCLUS: —if I'd known someone was already here. There's a cat?

ACHILLES: I call them Peleus.

PATROCLUS: Oh.

ACHILLES: Maybe they only come around when I'm in here. I think it's probably because usually I bring them my lunch after school.

PATROCLUS: I'm really sorry, I knew there was someone else coming here a lot but I just figured if I'd never seen them before then we probably wouldn't cross paths.

ACHILLES: I'm here every Tuesday. You've never been here on a Tuesday. How did you know?

PATROCLUS: What?

ACHILLES: That someone else came here.

PATROCLUS: [*confused*] Because the robot keeps putting on weight.

ACHILLES: Oh. Yeah he does. That's a weird way to put it, though.

PATROCLUS: Did you build him?

ACHILLES: Yes. He's not a robot, he's a machine. Well, he doesn't *go*, so I guess he's neither. He's just a—a friend.

PATROCLUS: A friend. How?

ACHILLES: He lets me talk to him. He lets me figure things out, when my head gets messy.

PATROCLUS: Aren't you, like—?

ACHILLES: Seventeen? Yeah, I am.

PATROCLUS: I didn't think seventeen year olds had imaginary friends.

ACHILLES: Well, see, he's not imaginary. [*Patting the machine's 'shoulder'*]. He's right here. Just because he can't like, speak out loud doesn't make him not real.

PATROCLUS: Yeah …

ACHILLES: I made him, that makes him real. For me.

PATROCLUS: You're right.

ACHILLES: I built him because I wanted to build a thing that would do what I say and love me and not leave.

PATROCLUS: And he can't leave if he's not alive.

ACHILLES: *No*, he can't leave because his legs don't work. You don't get it. I shouldn't be telling you this. Who even are you?

PATROCLUS: I'm sorry.

ACHILLES: I know he's not *real* real. Jesus. I'm not delusional. Isn't it just *nicer* if you pretend like he is? Like he can talk and stuff? Even if you know he can't? Isn't it nicer to pretend he's still here because he *chose* to be and not because he's incapable of moving? Why is it a crime to want him to be real?

PATROCLUS: You're right.

ACHILLES: And now you think I'm crazy.

PATROCLUS: No I don't.

ACHILLES: You think I'm weird.

> *Pause.*

PATROCLUS: A bit.

ACHILLES: I'm not, like, autistic or whatever. Or a sociopath. It's not like I think that's how human beings are supposed to work. Y'know, I'm not like, 'Ooh, build a robot because I can't deal with reality'. Why am I telling you any of this?

PATROCLUS: I didn't think you were.

ACHILLES: But you do think I'm weird.

> PATROCLUS *is silent.* ACHILLES *turns back to his machine, polishing a smudge.*

PATROCLUS: Maybe. I am autistic, though.

ACHILLES: Really?

PATROCLUS: Kinda, yeah.

ACHILLES: Oh. How?

PATROCLUS: I can't read analog clocks or sit still, and I say weird things sometimes, and I need to get changed each time I start a new activity.

ACHILLES: Seriously? How do you manage at school?

PATROCLUS: [*like it's obvious*] School only counts as one activity.

ACHILLES: Ah.

PATROCLUS: I'm not a sociopath either.

ACHILLES: I didn't think you were. That's not what I meant when I— see, now you think I'm a jerk. You think I'm an asshole who hates autistics and talks to himself.

PATROCLUS: No. I don't think that.

ACHILLES: Yeah if you say so. How did you get here?

PATROCLUS: Oh! Um. I only found it a couple of months ago. I was looking for locations for my vis art major work and I ended up here.

ACHILLES: I've been coming here since last year. I was walking home one afternoon and I saw Peleus. They let me chase them all the way down here, like it was a game and they wanted me to follow. I come here on Tuesdays after school, and on the weekend when I'm meant to be at saxophone lessons. My parents think I go to saxophone and instead I come here and then spend the money on iTunes vouchers.

PATROCLUS: Oh.

ACHILLES: Yeah I've kind of made it my own, y'know. All the others at school go to Starlight Plaza after school, or the library that used to be the church, and I get to come here and none of *them* will ever get to come here. I'm gonna move here after I graduate.

PATROCLUS: Can you actually do that?

ACHILLES: Who cares? Someone used to live here, at the very least. There's like half a mouldy couch in that pile over there. There used to be a little portable hot plate but I turned it into pectorals.

PATROCLUS: The robot, sorry, machine, wasn't here the first time. That I was here, I mean. When I came back after the first time he was here. It didn't feel right to use him for VA because someone else made him. Maybe now that you're here I could though?

ACHILLES: No.

PATROCLUS: Why not?

ACHILLES: He's not an artwork.

PATROCLUS: But he is, though, he's beautiful.

ACHILLES: He's not art, he's my friend.

PATROCLUS: Yeah, but—

ACHILLES: He's mine, he's not your ticket to a Band Six or whatever.

PATROCLUS: I'm sorry. I won't.

ACHILLES: You put him in your thing, your art thing, and everyone will come here to find him and everyone will know this place is here, and someone will turn it into a shitty hipster cafe or some shit, and then I'll be the robot-building crazy kid *and* I'll be homeless. Jesus.

PATROCLUS: I'm sorry, I'm sorry. I didn't understand. I would never, without permission, I wouldn't just take without asking. I'm sorry.

A silence. ACHILLES *considers* PATROCLUS. PATROCLUS *dissolves.*

ACHILLES: Okay. Don't freak out, or whatever.

Pause.

His name's Mojo.

PATROCLUS: [*looking up*] The robot?

ACHILLES: Like on the wall.

He points to 'PRAY 4 MOJO'.

PATROCLUS: Did you paint that?

ACHILLES: No, that's always been here. No idea what it means but it sounds cool.

PATROCLUS: Pray for Mojo.

ACHILLES: All hail Mojo.

> PATROCLUS *laughs for the first time. It seems to take both* ACHILLES *and* PATROCLUS *himself by surprise. His laugh is a clear, crisp peal.* ACHILLES *is captivated by it.*

PATROCLUS: All hail Mojo. [*Giggling again*] All hail Mojo. Sorry. That was funny.

ACHILLES: [*smiling*] I'm glad. That wasn't even my best. People don't think I'm very funny. But if you liked that then you'll probably love my best.

PATROCLUS: I don't think I find things funny properly? I laugh at the wrong stuff and I don't laugh at the right stuff. It's a whole, y'know, wonky brain thing.

ACHILLES: Well no-one else thinks I'm very funny so maybe I'm just as bad as you.

Pause; then a test.

Pass me that spring-y looking thing? Just behind your left foot.

> PATROCLUS *picks up the spring and brings it to* ACHILLES.

It's gonna be an antenna thing. The idea was that he'd use it to scan for nearby life forms and alert me to intruders, but I'm thinking maybe I just want him to be able to stab stuff with it. So you go to North Sydney Girls?

PATROCLUS: What? No. Why would you think that?

ACHILLES: You're still holding your blazer.

PATROCLUS: Shit. No, I do. I—ah. I go to North Sydney Girls, but I'm not, ummm … Not a girl.

ACHILLES: You're not a girl.

PATROCLUS: No.

ACHILLES: You're a boy?

PATROCLUS: Yes.

ACHILLES: Oh. So what's that like?

PATROCLUS: [*surprised by the lack of strong reaction*] Um? It's ... um, it feels like chewing aluminium foil, mostly.

ACHILLES: Huh. Well, apparently I'm a fag, so.

PATROCLUS: Oh, right.

ACHILLES: And my best friend is a robot who doesn't go, so you're in good company. Or bad company. Whatever.

PATROCLUS: What do you mean apparently?

ACHILLES: My mate Dino said I was. As a joke. Didn't feel incorrect. But I dunno.

PATROCLUS: The guy who invented the computer was gay.

ACHILLES: What?

PATROCLUS: Alan Turing, the inventor of the—

ACHILLES: Yeah, yeah, I know who you're talking about. Why would you say that?

PATROCLUS: You like machines. I just meant it's an alright thing to be. If you are. And alright if you're not, as well.

> *Pause.*

ACHILLES: Wasn't he autistic too?

PATROCLUS: Probably.

> ACHILLES *stares silently at* PATROCLUS *for a long moment.* PATROCLUS *squirms under the eye contact.*

What are you doing?

ACHILLES: Why are you still here?

PATROCLUS: Would you like me to go?

ACHILLES: I mean you've got your answer, you found the mysterious robot guy, you don't have to stick around.

PATROCLUS: If you want me to go I'll go now—

ACHILLES: Most people don't tolerate my company for this long.

PATROCLUS: I'm sorry, I can make sure I don't come here on Tuesday anymore—

ACHILLES: Also this place is creepy and enclosed—

PATROCLUS: —Or at all, if you want, I can go right now, I'm really sorry—

ACHILLES: —And you're alone with a weird guy who talks to imaginary robots. At the very least you've got to be thinking about how you're gonna gossip to your friends about me tomorrow.

PATROCLUS: I don't gossip.

ACHILLES: Then why are you still here?

PATROCLUS: [*searching wildly for a reason*] His nose.

ACHILLES: What?

PATROCLUS: His nose, he doesn't have one. [*Casting around for something, picking up a large bolt*] Here!

ACHILLES: Ooh. Uh, actually that's going to be his dick.

PATROCLUS: Oh.

ACHILLES: It's alright. Give me that. His dick can go on now. If you're staying, you better make yourself useful.

Blueberry Girl Grows Up

Ang Collins

BLUEBERRY GIRL *stands square on, centre stage. She's wearing a voluminous spherical blueberry costume, complete with little stalk hat.*

BLUEBERRY GIRL: Dad's got prostate cancer *and* bipolar.

He walks around the house naked with a cannula sticking out the top of his wrist.

You try to keep your head in your maths homework but it's kind of hard when there's a big hairy naked man in front of you chugging full cream milk like he's going for the world record.

Dad wears a gorilla mask to scare the shit out of Mum every day when she comes home from work. Mum goes angry and quiet but you think it's pretty fuckin' funny. Dave the old fat lab barks at Mum. Dad's out of breath for a half hour afterwards.

Dad spends half the day as a kid and half the day as an old man. You feel somewhere in between.

—

After school Thursday you go down the public pool with the boys from the boarding school—they bring their fancy wireless speakers and a box of Maxibons.

You lie on the grass next to the fifty-metre in your white bikini listening to Pink Floyd, which Brandon *really* wants everyone to listen to.

Wish You Were Here licks over you as the sky turns pink and white. Brandon yells the lyrics. Jono's looking at you. You think about Jono a lot.

You avoid his gaze and look down his flat chest and tummy instead. It's all silky marble in the warm dying light.

You adjust the left boob of your bikini suggestively.

Later Jono follows you to the girls' toilet block, past the pointed looks of Brandon and the other boys. Jono grabs your hand and scoops the back of your neck as he pulls your nose to his.

Inserts his tongue into your mouth.

You kiss back out of shock and he tumble dries inside your jaw and your heart jumps with thrill and discomfort and then he leaves you and that's your first real kiss.

—

Dad's off work but his new passion is *hot sauce*. Friday Mum drives Dad to Woolies so he can look at the hot sauce in the international aisle. He crouches down and religiously reads the back of every brand:
red chilli pepper powder refined sugar tomato purée eleven calories per hundred gram serving total fat zero-point-four grams apple cider vinegar salt water chemicals chemicals fuckin' chemicals BLAZIN' HOT!

Mum works her way round the store, leaving Dad to his own devices.

She's tired a lot but she doesn't complain.

Dad buys *all* the bottles of hot sauce in the international aisle of Woolies. He buys oyster sauce and Tabasco too. Tells Mum he's going to make his own.

'Too much bloody chemicals in these ones.'

Mum nods and says nothing.

You want Dad to get better.

—

You chew absently on your silverside and broccoli. Dad cleans out the bottles of Tabasco and chilli and oyster and dumps all the sauce into the sink. Red and black swirling liquid galaxy incrementally sucked down the wormhole of the kitchen sink.

'Looks like your first period, doesn't it lovie! You were twelve and bawlin' your eyes out and how gross did it smell!'

Dad slips a fingertip of sink Tabasco to Dave the old fat lab. Dave hacks and coughs for the whole night:

hack hack hack

Dave stands next to your bed, hacking at you in the dark.

You think about Jono's brown stripy irises and you feel a faint pulse inside your undies.

—

Dad has a bed day Saturday and shaves his eyebrows off.

You brush eyebrow hairs off the doona into your palm and wash them down the sink.

Dad flicks his cannula.

'Wish *I* was goin' out tonight.'

It's Jono's eighteenth tonight and you're going as a blueberry because the theme is 'childhood memories' and you want to look like Violet Beauregarde from Willy Wonka but sluttier.

This is the most make-up you've ever worn and you're self-conscious that the mineral foundation you bought is a shade too orange for your pale skin, and you can still see the freckles on your nose.

The party's mostly girls from the private school and boarders drinking vodka slopped into chocolate Oak cartons and you feel like their eyes are on you as they scream at each other to chug.

You cling to the small group of townies and nip little swigs of Johnnie Walker someone stole from Jono's dad's cabinet.

You're too nervous to talk to Jono, who's dressed in a pink fairy costume and is slumped wide-legged on his back deck, leaning back into the lap of a girl with dirty blonde hair and big boobs, who you decide you don't like. He looks over his shoulder and grins drunkenly, lifting his weight from the deck and gliding to the townie congregation.

He takes you upstairs and he tumble dries your mouth again and then you

kind of

awkwardly

wriggle out of your blueberry costume, leaving it slumped in a heap on the floor and you stand holding yourself in a lacy bralette that you bought at Kmart the day before.

And your saggy Bonds undies.

And you show each other yours and you decide a penis looks really fucking weird. You touch it and hold it, feel the weight of it in your cupped hand.

He makes a choked and with a morbid curiosity you watch as ejaculate spews out the tip right onto your palm, like a hose you're turning on at the rusty old backyard tap.

He apologises over and over and says 'I really like you.'

—

You're drunk and you go for a smoke behind Starlight Plaza with Brandon and the boys. You buy hot chips from the chicken shop for the cool walk home. You eat them all in maybe two minutes and feel guilty straight away.

You tuck your arms into your big blueberry body to keep warm. A big plump purple armless blob roaming the suburbs.

Breath of potato and cigarettes and you forget about your mum's glassy blue eyes and the wet in your underpants.

You look up at the grey late-night sky—not dark and crisp, but heavy-hanging; a lumpy canopy of charcoal cloud.

You walk toward a glowing oblong of familiar yellow canary light.

Front door's open.

You can already hear Dad shouting, muffled and distorted by the plaster corners of the house.

Hot sauce bottles all over the kitchen floor. Living room carpet patched with psychedelic orange globs; liquid over-saturating in places, smooth red-orange sitting atop the fuzz.

Dad's bellowing something; you hop to the hallway and there they are: Mum curled up against the door of the linen closet with her head down and Dad wailing incomprehensible obscenities, harsh and animal.

His body's stiff and his fingers crumple in and out with a violent tension, and he looks at nothing but his eyes are wide.

Fixed on one spot on the wall and screaming at it with so much *anger* and so much *pain*, and his eyes find you and try to speak out against the screams.

Tears are welling up in two glistening semi-circles under his bulging eyes and he's got a big glob of snot in the centre fold above his top lip.

And he's just going and going and yelling for Mum to get the fuck out and you get on top of him and you *hit him* and *hit him* and tell him to shut the fuck up.

Dave the old fat lab barks at Dad, short sharp snarls curling his jowls before he sounds.

You leap off Dad and grab Mum's arms, pressing your fingers in with an attempt at a reassuring force, and you lift her up like you're some kind of superhero in a blueberry costume, and you push her out the door, out the gate.

There's a bubbling up in your throat—hot sauce—and chilli gas streaming out your eyes and off your tongue up into the night sky.

You keep walking, down the street, through the park where the mist hangs above the grass, past Jono's house where the lights are still on.

You growl softly at Mum:

don't stop don't stop don't you dare stop.

And she doesn't.

Twin

Louis Klee

LENA, K *and* ANDREW, *all seventeen. Once onstage, the characters remain in the space even when not speaking or involved in the action.*

LENA: I made you cookies.

> *Pause.*

Used your oven. I hope you don't mind. Just found a big sausage of cookie dough in the fridge.

[*Off* K*'s reaction*] What?

K: Nothing. Could've asked.

LENA: Wouldn't have been a surprise then, would it?

K: I buy it because I like it raw.

LENA: That's *rank*.

K: It just doesn't taste as good cooked. As raw.

LENA: Okay.

> *Pause.*

You in a bad mood or something?

K: No.

LENA: In a funk. You're grumpy.

K: I'm not grumpy.

LENA: What were you watching?

> *Silence.*

Just then I came in. You were watching something.

K: Oh. Just this stupid thing for English.

> *Pause.*

Why?

LENA: You minimised it.

K: No I didn't.

LENA: You did. When you heard me, you minimised it.

K: So?

LENA: Then maximise it. / Now.

K: No.

> *Silence.*

You think it was porn?

LENA: Well … was it?

K: Would you be jealous?

LENA: You don't watch porn.

K: How do you know?

LENA: I just *know.*

K: Oh yeah? You still cut up that I didn't want to watch that thing with you? Lesbians fucking each other's brains out?

LENA: It was just a bit of / fun!

K: You still *fuming* about that?

LENA: I was never fuming about that.

K: Oh so you just happened to say you think I'm asexual to—

LENA: I never said—can we just *not*—

K: Yeah. Let's not.

> *Silence.*

LENA: What was with the hood?

K: What hood?

LENA: In the video. He was wearing a / hood.

K: It's just some clip. From a band I like.

LENA: The sound was off.

K: I mean—what? Why do you even care?

LENA: What was he doing in the quadrangle?

K: Waiting? I don't know.

LENA: To have his head sliced off.

> *Beat.*

Why were you watching a beheading? [*To* ANDREW] A beheading.

ANDREW: Jesus.

LENA: I hope it's not weird that I'm here—

ANDREW: You're trembling.

LENA: Just tell me if—

ANDREW: You're shaking.

LENA: It's that—

ANDREW: It's fine! Just sit down on the bed already.

> *Beat.*

LENA: Thanks.

ANDREW: Breathe.

LENA: I just can't get the image out of my head—

ANDREW: In and out—

LENA: The way the blade just clean diced—

ANDREW: [*squeamish*] Okay, okay!

> *Pause.*

I'm / sorry.

LENA: No, sorry.

ANDREW: I'm sorry about that.

LENA: Why are you sorry?

ANDREW: It's just a phase. I think. He's curious.

LENA: About beheadings?

ANDREW: Yeah.

> *Pause.*

No, you're right—yeah, he's fucked in the head. Are you smiling?

LENA: No.

ANDREW: Why are you smiling?

LENA: I'm / not.

ANDREW: You're laughing!

LENA: I can't help it! I—it's just—

ANDREW: What?

LENA: You. You two. Spitting image. It's like you're him talking to me about himself. Which he would *never* do.

> *Pause.*

Could you be any more different? For twins, I / mean.

ANDREW: I get it.

LENA: Only seconds between you. That's it—seconds. Everything else the same. Same house. Same books. Same height. Eyes—*your* eyes. Even your mum can't tell you apart in photos. The way she pauses. Before she points out who's who. I can tell she's making it up. She gets it wrong even. Sometimes it's him holding the snowball. Other times it's—Andrew? Are you / listening?

ANDREW: [*To* K] I said are you listening to me?

    K *is silent.*

I just—
  I—
  Pause.

How could you do that to her? Like, are you crazy? You're lucky to have a girl who actually gives a fuck about you and you—you dump her?

K: I didn't—

ANDREW: Oh, *come on!*

K: I didn't dump her. Jeez. She just gets on my nerves, okay? Why do you even care?

ANDREW: Because I'm your—

K: Can you just get out my room?

ANDREW: No. You're going to listen to me because *I* had to take the flack. For you. Said sorry. For you. Begged her to forgive you *like I was you.* I don't want to have to do that—

K: Yeah and I don't want you to do that. I never asked you to / do that.

ANDREW: Shut up for a minute, alright? Sometimes I don't get it. You've got so much potential. That's what makes this sad. Just like … get off your arse. For once try and be more an entrepreneur with life. It's like you just think you can brood away in this mess eating—what even is this? And / everyone will just come cleaning up after you. Come running after you. I've got news for you. Life doesn't work like—

K: It's loading. Slower now I've cranked the resolution right up: one thousand, two hundred and eighty by one thousand and twenty-four.

ANDREW: Take your fucking headphones out.

    Pause.

Look at / me!

K: Up early. Looking. For something that seems really *real*—the way they did the water effects—the ocean—the sheer perfection of that slight shimmer—yellow … no, *orange* on the cusp of dark waves when afternoon light catches the swell. They did that with a few pixels. Hard to believe. Up close just squares. One colour each square …

LENA: Yeah …

K: Yeah.

LENA: And?

K: You see it?

LENA: Well yeah but *who cares?* If you like waves so much we could go to an *actual* beach?

K: I think you're missing the point.

LENA: How?

K: You like *art*, don't you? Looking at a painting of a beach? Don't you?

LENA: It's not the same as some *game!* It's not the same. He's not the same anyone. And it just makes me think …

ANDREW: Yeah?

LENA: I shouldn't say this.

> *Pause.*

ANDREW: Are you actually not saying it?

LENA: No.

ANDREW: Wow, you're such a tease!

LENA: Oh, shut up.

> *Beat.*

It makes me think it's you.

ANDREW: But you know I—

LENA: Can you let me finish—

> *Pause.*

That, well, the things I thought I saw in him—*liked* in him—were really the things that remind me of you … There. I said it.

> *Pause.*

You ignore me … next to him in bed and he's on his phone like I'm not even there. Watching some video on his phone and I press my foot. Up his thigh I press my foot. Up his boxer / shorts.

K: Can you just—

LENA: What?

> *Pause.*

I brush my toes against his / cock.

K: I know what you're / doing.

LENA: And it's like … *nothing*. Watching his video and I know he can hear me next to him. / Breathing.

K: Panting next / to me.

LENA: Masturbating.

K: It's the video I can't hear.

LENA: Just chooses to ignore / me.

K: If I'm not replying to your texts it's because I don't *feel* like replying to your / texts.

LENA: But I go round anyway and before I'm through his door he's ranting about *you*, Andrew, his 'gay left-wing sissy communist brother', who 'doesn't understand *the way of the world*, how things *just are*, you can't change it, that's *the way the world is*—'. Turning on me, bad-mouthing *feminism* and the *twitterati*. I don't even use / Twitter.

K: Twitter is a tool of public shaming. A reversion to village politics. The lefty lynch mob—

LENA: Oh, what would you know? Do you even use / Twitter?

K: Oh, I see. You think I don't *understand*. I can't understand your experience because you're just so different.

LENA: I never said anything about experience. When did I ever say anything about my experience?

K: I'm mansplaining?

LENA: What does that even mean—

K: Do you want me to—

ANDREW: Yes. Please explain.

    Silence.

'FAGGOT'. You don't just write that on your own brother's—

    He breaks off.

On your own brother's door. You just don't—

    Pause.

Say something. For fuck's sake. Anything.

K: One at a time. In big black letters. Thought I was going to write 'FUCK' … but after the F it just came out: 'FAGGOT'.

ANDREW: I know you and Lena. You're finished. Or whatever. I / know—

LENA: You won't know him.

K: Then it won't matter if you tell me.

Pause.

You could tell me his first name. Just his …

LENA: Don't make this any harder.

ANDREW: I know you're going to say no, but just hear me out. Soon school's done. Finished. We can go anywhere. Russia, Argentina, Turkey—whatever.

Pause.

LENA: Eyob.

K: Eyob? I know Eyob.

LENA: You don't.

K: I do. I know him.

LENA: This is pathetic.

K: He won that thing. That prize.

LENA: *You don't know him!*

K: The—the flutist—

LENA: Flautist.

Beat.

Yeah. That's him.

K:

ANDREW: I just booked it. The Golan Heights. Hiking. You and I. I know you *think* you're scared of planes but it's really not that bad.

K: It's the glitches I like, where the physics break down.

ANDREW: But you haven't even been on a plane. How can you be scared of something if you've never even experienced it?

K: The bits that the game's designers have neglected. The bits they've fucked up and haven't patched yet. The bits where if you hit the right buttons in quick succession the whole thing goes, like, epileptic and you float there with your legs still moving as if you're walking but underneath you there's nothing.

The Arcade

Lewis Treston

The arcade is alive with a carnival of peculiar, dissonant and beautiful sounds. KAROLINA, a German exchange student, wears an eighties-inspired formal dress with Converse shoes. She watches as STUART, also dressed in formal attire, removes his jacket and delicately hangs it over the railing in front.

KAROLINA: So what are the rules?

STUART: … See those red targets?

KAROLINA: No.

STUART: They're small but they're everywhere. There's one on that owl's left wing.

KAROLINA: Yes. I see it, I see it—so how do you win?

STUART: Right. All the different targets have different points, so—yeah … The trickier the target the more points you get and one point equals one ticket—

KAROLINA: Tickets?

STUART: Like, little paper stub things—

KAROLINA: I know what tickets are but where do we get the tickets from?

STUART: There are no physical tickets. There used to be real tickets though. They'd come spitting out of the machine and I'd keep them all in my pencil case. They still say tickets at the prize counter though.

KAROLINA: Ergh! English makes no sense.

STUART: But different games have a different ratio from points to tickets—some games you earn like thousands of points but it only / equates to ten tickets …

KAROLINA: I understand. The ratio of points to tickets is one to one—so what do we do with the tickets?

STUART: Well, we exchange them for an any one of a number of spectacular prizes. I want the slime-green lava lamp.

KAROLINA: … And how many tickets is that?

STUART: Two thousand.

KAROLINA: Two thousand …! Fine. So we get the slime green lava lamp then we can go back?

STUART: Go back?

KAROLINA: Yes. Go back to the formal.

STUART: … You want to go back?

KAROLINA: Of course …

STUART swipes his pre-paid arcade card before picking up the plastic rifle and begins to take aim at a target in front. His gaze narrows. He puts his finger on the trigger. He realigns the shot. He furrows his brow. He squeezes the trigger just the tiniest bit, until:

Just take the shot.

STUART: Shh … I'm becoming a man.

KAROLINA: What are you aiming at?

STUART: The owl.

KAROLINA: No. No, leave the owl out of this … Shoot the cans.

STUART: It's a fake owl. The cans are real though.

KAROLINA: Really I had no idea.

STUART: It's like an animatronic owl—

KAROLINA: I was being sarcastic—

STUART: … Really?

KAROLINA: Yes, I know, with my accent sarcasm isn't easy to—err— isn't easy to—what's the word … Oh my God—what is it …? See, I'm flustered now …

STUART: Isn't easy to pick up on?

KAROLINA: Yes. 'Pick up on'. Understand. Comprehend.

She watches STUART as he continues to painstakingly line up the shot.

Oh! Just shoot. It isn't going anywhere.

STUART fires the plastic rifle and it emits a tinny electronic blast. A pause.

Did you hit it?

STUART: No … The owl normally hoots a little bit when you shoot it.

KAROLINA: Oh, yes! Of course. The owl just hoots a little in protest when you shoot it with a rifle.

STUART: / Fake owl. Fake rifle.

KAROLINA: [*doing an incensed owl impression*] 'Hoot! Hoot! You've shot my hoot!'

STUART: … See, that was better. Subtle commentary on gun violence combined with an owl impression. Dripping with sarcasm with a nearly perfect landing. Difficulty ten.

KAROLINA: My landing was perfect …

> KAROLINA *touches* STUART *on the forearm before taking the plastic rifle off him. She takes aim, focuses on her target for a few seconds, before rapidly firing five times, hitting the same target in quick succession. It's impressive.*

STUART: Where did you learn to shoot?

KAROLINA: My grandparents were Nazis.

STUART: … Are you allowed to joke about that?

KAROLINA: I'm not joking … [*Grinning*] Australians are so funny—

STUART: I don't get it.

KAROLINA: I shot five cans—how many points is that?

STUART: Twenty-five points. Twenty-five tickets.

KAROLINA: Twenty-five? But those five shots cost two dollars.

STUART: Yes, it's one dollar for the tickets and one extra dollar for all the fun you're supposed to be having.

KAROLINA: [*seriously*] I am having fun. [*Taking aim*] Where's that owl gone?

STUART: [*pointing*] There.

> KAROLINA *fires rapidly: she is less successful this time.*

KAROLINA: Shit!

STUART: Close.

KAROLINA: [*inspecting the rifle*] The barrel on this thing is all bent. How are / you supposed to …

STUART: Don't stress.

KAROLINA: I'm not stressed I just hate losing.

> *She tries to bend it back into shape for a moment, then gives up.*

Have you ever thought about just buying the lava lamp?

STUART: You can go back if you want …

KAROLINA: ... Well of course I can go back if I want ... Do you want me to go?

STUART: I'm just saying, don't feel like you have to stay just because I'm here ... [*Cannot let it go*] Were your grandparents actually Nazis?

KAROLINA: My grandparents weren't Nazis ... Stuart—

STUART: [*mimicking*] Karolina.

STUART *tries to take the plastic rifle from* KAROLINA *but she refuses to relinquish it.*

KAROLINA: Stuart ... What do you think I'm thinking?

STUART: What are you thinking?

KAROLINA: Yes.

STUART: ... Why are you asking me?

KAROLINA: Just tell me what you think I'm thinking.

STUART: ... You're thinking about how you're going to get me to go back to the formal ... Am I right?

KAROLINA: ... Are you feeling any better?

STUART: Fine.

KAROLINA: Have you calmed down?

STUART: I feel fine. I've felt fine all night. Now what were you thinking?

KAROLINA: ... I was asking myself if it's a secret why I'm here.

STUART *takes the plastic rifle, painstakingly lines up his shot and fires three times.*

STUART: So that's about a hundred tickets. Only / one thousand nine...

KAROLINA: Why am I here? Stuart. Tell me.

STUART: ... I didn't ask you to come—

KAROLINA: You said, 'Let's go.' How is that not an invitation? If anything it's an instruction. You told me to leave with you.

STUART: I didn't feel like dancing—

KAROLINA: You went white ... Actually you've been white all night, but, yeah—you went whiter once they turned the music on ... Is whiter a word?

STUART: ... No—

KAROLINA: What do you mean no?

STUART: No, whiter isn't a word ... Actually, no, it is—isn't it?

KAROLINA: Your chest was rattling like one of those wind up toys that spin and buzz around on the ground like it was having a seizure—

STUART: [*glibly*] What toy is that?

KAROLINA: You were literally shaking! So I came over and you looked at me straight in the eyes for a change and said, 'Let's go.'

STUART: … Yeah, but that doesn't mean you had to come—

KAROLINA: Then what does it mean? What? Tell me what that means so I can leave.

STUART: Go dance! Really, I mean it—go have the best time tonight and I'll see you when—when … When will I see you?

KAROLINA: Saturday.

STUART: What are we doing Saturday?

KAROLINA: Saturday—I leave on Saturday. I told you this.

STUART: Really? This Saturday?

KAROLINA: … Yes. I'm flying Sydney to Hong Kong, then Hong Kong to London, then I'm … I'm actually going to spend three nights and four days in London. Then it's back to Berlin.

STUART: Really?

Pause.

KAROLINA: Yes.

STUART: So what are you going to do in London?

KAROLINA: Theatre … galleries … that kind of thing. So this is it.

She takes the gun from STUART *but does nothing with it.*

So …

STUART: Did I say I liked your dress?

KAROLINA: [*smiling*] No. You didn't but thank you. When I go home I have to go to my proper school formal. Mum has already picked out my real dress. I prefer this hideous thing though.

STUART: It's not hideous.

KAROLINA: You're right, that is the wrong word … I don't know—what would you say?

STUART: About the dress? It's sort of … wacky, but … yeah, no—I'm just going to settle on wacky.

KAROLINA: Wacky … and the shoes?

STUART: Comfortable.

KAROLINA: Comfortably wacky. I like that.

STUART: Do you like the tie?

KAROLINA: I do … I like the fishes.

STUART: My sister gives me lots of ties …
KAROLINA: … Okay.
STUART: She said she got this one in Camden Markets actually. In London … You'll have to go there and look at the ties.
KAROLINA: I can send you one back if you like?
STUART: No. No point. This is the first time I've worn one all year. My collection is huge though but—yeah, it's kind of meaningless.
KAROLINA: I'm going to buy you the wackiest tie you can imagine. And one day, when you're an old man, you'll be picking up your bran and milk from the Starlight Plaza and the girl at the checkout will ask, 'Where did you get that crazy tie?' and you'll say, 'Karolina bought it for me.'
STUART: Well if you want to—
KAROLINA: I do.

> KAROLINA *locks eyes with* STUART. *He doesn't look away. The incessant pinging and dinging of the arcade fills the electric silence shared between them.*

> KAROLINA *takes a step closer and reaches for his hand.*

STUART: … Is it my turn or yours?
KAROLINA: [*handing* STUART *the rifle*] Yours.
STUART: … This place used to be my day care. Dad would drop me and my brothers and sister off and we'd just stay here all day shooting and whacking stuff. We'd redeem all types of stuff with the ticket but we'd normally just end up getting these bouncy balls though. You know those rubber little bouncy balls? We'd take them out to the carpark and we'd just watch them fly. Dozens of these tiny stupid coloured balls just zipping smashing against the asphalt in every direction … One time one of the balls cracked someone's rearview mirror … The manager told my Dad we weren't allowed to come back for a while.
KAROLINA: … I think I'm going to go.
STUART: What about the slime green lava lamp?
KAROLINA: Yeah, best of luck with that—
STUART: Karolina, wait … We could get bouncy balls. We could redeem hundreds of bouncy balls, take them back to the formal and just watch shit fly!

KAROLINA: … What are you talking about? Bouncy balls …? How obvious do I need to be? There is a procedure for things like this. I've made my intentions clear and either you reciprocate or you don't. Stop wasting my time as you try and make up your mind or find the nerve or whatever shit you're trying to work out … I'm going. Soon. For good … If you have any respect for me at all, please, please just tell me to go if you don't … If you don't. Stuart tell me so I can go and dance and sneak drinks with everyone else and actually enjoy my last few days here …

STUART: … I …

KAROLINA: Yes?

STUART: … I—err … I'm not very good at, you know, this kind of … And … Yeah—I'm not very good at that … What do you want me to say?

KAROLINA: … You know what? It doesn't matter.

> STUART, *without warning, approaches* KAROLINA *and kisses her on the mouth. It appears tender at first however as the kiss escalates it takes on a procedural grace. It's clinical, considered, with an air of obligation.* KAROLINA *allows the kiss to come to a premature end.*

STUART: … Is that what you wanted?

> KAROLINA *sort-of smiles, or does she nod?*

How do things already feel different?

KAROLINA: They're not. They are but they're—wait—what do you … Are you talking about us, or …?

STUART: I was looking forward to tonight—I just … It was like we were all pretending. Everyone had sort of adopted these new costumes and pretending we understood what they meant. Like we were suddenly in control of something inside of us that we weren't given access to before … I wanted to stay, and dance, and just go along with everything that tonight is about, but … I just wanted to do something that made sense. So I came here … And I guess you came with me.

KAROLINA: … I'm going to go back.

STUART: Really? You're not going to help me win the lava lamp?

> KAROLINA *gives a small laugh.*

KAROLINA: No. Definitely not ... I guess this is another goodbye moment ... I've done them so many times this week, but, yes ... Goodbye Stuart.

STUART: ... Maybe I'll see you Saturday. I could come to the airport.

KAROLINA: Maybe, yeah.

STUART: Karolina ...

KAROLINA: Yes?

STUART: ... Nothing ... I'll see ya later.

KAROLINA *smiles softly and exits.* STUART, *without interruption, picks up the plastic rifle, takes aim and fires, once, twice, three times, then again and again and again and again ... The tinny sound of the plastic gun finds its place in the cacophony of manic arcade noises.*

Dive

Izzy McDonald

BILL, *a seventeen-year-old boy, sits on top of the hill. Not a mountain. He is not wearing a suit. The light is yellow and the air is wet. It's always wet here.*

JERRY, *a seventeen-year-old girl, makes a puffed entry. Ball gown on. High heels in hand.* BILL *stands as she enters. They stare at each other. Stillness.*

BILL: What are you doing here?

JERRY: What are you doing here?

BILL: What are *you* doing here? Tonight?

JERRY: I wanted to come here?

BILL: Well, you're here. Now you can go.

JERRY: Oh piss in the gutter and swim, this isn't yours.

BILL: Um yes it is.

JERRY: You're not better than everyone else. Just because you didn't go.

BILL: Neither are you.

JERRY: Good call.

BILL: You obviously wanted to.

JERRY: [*looking her very-dressed self up and down*] Obviously. I changed my mind, okay?

BILL: Okay.

> *Pause.*

JERRY: Everyone looked ugly.

> BILL *laughs.*

BILL: You're deep.

JERRY: Not their dresses. Or suits. It was just ugly, ya know? My dress has too much glitter on it. Why does every thing need so much glitter tonight?

BILL: It's the one night they get to feel shiny I spose. Like shiny things.

JERRY: I don't want to be a shiny thing.

Pause.

BILL: You should go back. You don't want to be here.

JERRY: I'm never coming back.

BILL: Where?

JERRY: Here.

BILL: My hill?

JERRY: Again, it's not yours. And no I don't mean Couch Hill. I mean Peakings.

Pause.

BILL: You leaving?

JERRY: Yep.

BILL: Where?

JERRY: North. Dry. No ocean.

BILL: What does your mum think?

JERRY: [*ignoring the question*] I don't want to smell it anymore.

BILL: The ocean? Mum reckons it's stuck in her nose for good.

JERRY: I need to move. Not like, spread out. Not stretch. Move. I don't think I've ever moved. Forwards, backwards, sideways. It's more, it's more, floating. Like a buoy in water.

BILL: Like a body?

JERRY: No. Like a buoy. One of those balls that fisherman use to mark out a path. I think.

BILL: Kinda like the pontoon?

JERRY: Kinda like the pontoon. You never know if it's coming towards you or not. It's bobbles, sways but never moves. Always floating, never moving. Just sitting there, confusing you. Anchored to the bottom of the ocean. Stuck there. I am so sick of floating.

Silence.

I've always been good at floating. Mum reckons when I step in the water, all the salt, from the entire world, steps in with me. And I just stay on top.

BILL: I can't dive.

JERRY: Oh?

BILL: Just can't do it.

JERRY: It's not that hard.

BILL: It wouldn't be for you, would it?

JERRY: What's that supposed to—

BILL: —Forget it. Just rack off. Go back to it. Go back to the glitter and have fun.

JERRY: Why don't you?! Suck it up and put on a suit. Try a smile maybe. Even just for one photo? Or are you too much of a pussy?

She makes a camera with hands and clicks it.

Silence.

She lowers her hands, slowly.

Sorry. That was over the top.

Pause.

I can teach you?

BILL: What?

JERRY: To dive. When it gets hot again. If I'm still here.

BILL: Mum's tried to teach me every summer. When she dives it's, it's, phwoaaah. For a big woman she really nails it. I get the concept. I just can't do it. And if she can't teach me, you sure as fuck can't. Okay?

JERRY: [*laughing softly*] What happens when you try?

BILL: [*gesturing with hands*] SMACK.

JERRY: Ouch.

BILL: You?

JERRY: Ten out of ten, nothing but elegance here mate, perfect form.

BILL: Naturally.

Pause.

Don't you just float?

JERRY: I definitely don't stay down for long.

BILL: I sink. Down. I let all the air out of my lungs and I think I breathe big.

JERRY: What?

BILL inhales deeply and holds his breath while speaking:

BILL: Bigger than others.

JERRY: Alright, Big Man Bill. Let it out before you pass out.

BILL exhales a big breath.

BILL: The bubbles go above my head. Speak to the surface. I get to sink and the air can do the talking.

Pause.

I like that nickname more.

JERRY: What?

BILL: Big Man Bill. It's better than Bucktooth Bill.

JERRY: Why do they call you that?

BILL *points to his teeth. Very bucked.*

Right. Well. Who made it up?

BILL: Really?

Pause.

You did.

Pause.

We were kids. You didn't make the whole legend up. Or … what I did to her.

JERRY: I never believed that.

BILL: No shit. Doubt you'd be sitting here with me if you did.

JERRY: When did I call you that? I thought it was Brenda? Or Cass, or one of those girls.

BILL: Nah. Lets not do this okay?

JERRY: No. I want to know.

BILL: I don't want to talk about it with you.

JERRY: You're being a pussy again. I want to know!

BILL: And fuck what I want right?

JERRY: Sorry.

BILL: Sorry. I can't believe you don't remember. Alright. We were kids. Year two. Same class, remember?

Silence.

Jesus Christ. Well, we were. We were at the shops. Before Starlight Plaza had a Woolies. They had the black-and-white checked lino. And it always smelt like rotisserie chicken. Like, fucking always.

JERRY: Holy shit. Yes!

BILL: My mum ran the newsagency. Do you remember that? Your mum would always come and buy three scratchies and the *Sunday Times*, every Sunday.

JERRY: She still does that. Just at Woolies now, I suppose.

BILL: Yeah I think that's what everyone does now. Anyway, they would talk for hours. Even when other customers came in. And our mums would just talk and talk and talk. My mum would never talk to anyone like that. Not even me.

You'd race off to the skate park across the road. And I'd watch you. You owned it. Held it with everyone. I was kind of in awe of you.

Your mum was crying one day. Her eye was bruised. And then my mum was crying. It was the first time I'd seen two grownups cry together.

And she didn't want you to race off to the skate park. She wanted you nearby. Close to her. So you went and sat on the stack of newspapers at the front of the store. Sulking. And staring out at the kids across at the park. And that's what I would always do and suddenly you were in my spot. You were just like me. Stuck in a newsagency with your mum. Sulking.

JERRY: I remember that. I can't remember you being there. Like ever.

BILL: I came and sat on the stack next to you.

JERRY: Oh my God.

BILL: Oh, so there is a light in there.

JERRY: You tried to kiss me! But your teeth hit my cheek. Hard. I started to bleed a little I think.

BILL: It seemed like a lot.

JERRY: Is that when? When did I call you—

BILL: Never to my face. You ran out the door. Your mum yelled out to you but you didn't listen.

JERRY: Never did.

BILL: And you ran over and told everyone about how Bucktooth Bill tried to kiss you.

JERRY: I'm sorry.

BILL: It's just a name.

JERRY: I'm so sorry.

BILL: It's just a name.

JERRY: I never believed them.

BILL: Never? About how I took her? Hurt her? Buried her at the top of Couch Hill? How they found her necklace in my pencil case and that was enough proof. A two-dollar-shop piece of shit proves what I did? And you never believed them. The only reason we are talking is because of Miss Andrews. The assignment. That I practically did by myself by the way. We had that and the time I tried to kiss you when we were seven. That's it, Jerry. I'm sure you didn't believe any of it.

JERRY: I didn't.

BILL: Yeah well, I never believed them either.

JERRY: What?

BILL: What they said about your mum. That she deserved it. That she was a slut so she deserved to get a good slap.

JERRY: Fuck you.

BILL: What?

JERRY: You can't just say that. Saying it, repeating it, it's just as bad as fucking believing it.

BILL: I know.

Silence.

We were kids.

JERRY: Everyone thinks we still are.

BILL: I saw them holding hands once.

JERRY: Who?

BILL: Our mums.

JERRY: What?

BILL: They were holding hands across the counter. They didn't see me watching.

JERRY: Mum never held hands with Dad.

BILL: It was really gentle. They were playing. Like schoolgirls.

JERRY: Did you say anything?

BILL: Why would I?

JERRY: Because our mums were holding hands? Is that not weird to you?

BILL: It was weird. It was weird because Mum was so comfortable. She struggles with people, Mum. Not with me but with pretty much everyone else.

JERRY: We stopped going to the newsagency.

BILL: Yeah, I remember.

JERRY: Before Woolies moved into the Starlight.

BILL: Yeah, I remember.

JERRY: When Dad—

BILL: Mum closed up shop a month later. Could see the end coming, she reckons. But I knew they were kicking us out. Even then.

JERRY: That was bullshit what they did. Pushing you guys out. It was wrong what they did.

BILL: It *was*.

JERRY: It was wrong what I did. When we were kids.

Silence.

BILL: Why'd you come here? To my ... I mean, this spot.

JERRY: I needed somewhere to watch.

BILL: Watch what?

JERRY *points down to the water.*

The pontoon. It's on fire.

JERRY *nods. Stillness.*

Palaces of Montezuma

Peter Beaglehole

Late at night.

Not midnight.

Not yet.

HASSAN, HARPER *and* NADINE *are on a bridge, drinking, haloed by white headlights. They're dressed formally.* HASSAN *and* NADINE *wear borrowed clothes.* HARPER *does not.*

NADINE: Gross
HARPER: What?
HASSAN: Mossie

>   *She crushes it.*

NADINE: The blood
>   it's thick
HARPER: Congealed
HASSAN: Probably got AIDS
HARPER: Don't be an idiot
HASSAN: Joking
NADINE: No
>   No
>   It's on Mum's dress
HARPER: What else would you expect?
HASSAN: 'What else would you expect?'
>   Sound sour
HARPER: I'm not sour
NADINE: Bitter
HARPER: I'm not bitter.
>   I thought we'd go somewhere different.
NADINE: What for?
HARPER: We could do the same thing
>   somewhere else
NADINE: No.

This place is special.
Best spot for yabbies.
HASSAN: Not now
it's plastic and algae
HARPER: You sound sour
HASSAN: Dunno what you mean
NADINE: This year's important.
It won't be the same
this is the last chance
last time we'll all be here
HASSAN: No-one's dying
HARPER: I might visit
NADINE: Might?
HARPER: I will visit.
Next Christmas
NADINE: And New Year?
HASSAN: Yeah,
joined at the hip
right?
HARPER: Right.
NADINE: You two
are complete
dickheads

She sprays them both with drink from between her teeth.

Now we're matching
HARPER: Suits you better
HASSAN: You cunt
HARPER: Hey
HASSAN: Not funny
NADINE: It's fairly funny
HASSAN: Only white shirt I got
HARPER: I'll buy you a new one
NADINE: You can have one of my work shirts,
they're white
HASSAN: Girl's shirt wouldn't fit
HARPER: Have to fit better than
what you've got

HASSAN: It's alright

HARPER: You look like your dad

NADINE: How pissed was he?

HARPER: Enough to get grabby

HASSAN: Fuck off

NADINE: Keep the bottle away from this one.
    A late night with
    a pair of likely ladies

HASSAN: I'm not my old man

HARPER: No,
    she's right,
    it's in the blood.
    Best tipped in
    the river

NADINE: Stop.
    What are you doing?

HARPER: What?

NADINE: We finish it.
    Every year
    we finish it

HASSAN: Tasted bad

NADINE: That's our tradition,
    drink the wine
    jump in the river and swim

HARPER: We're not finishing it this year,
    you've already had plenty

NADINE: I'm fine

HARPER: That's the sign

NADINE: For what?

HASSAN: You'll black out
    lightweight

NADINE: I won't

HARPER: You will.
    You push it every time

HASSAN: Drink makes you sleepy

HARPER: It makes you angry

NADINE: Makes you more of a bitch.

HARPER: More?
HASSAN: Yeah
NADINE: You can be
   stand-offish
HARPER: Stand-offish?
NADINE: Cold.
HASSAN: Frigid.
   No love locks
   for you
NADINE: Don't see any locks for you Hassan.
   Marko and Nadine
   Steve and Nadine
   Jesse and Nadine
HASSAN: Marko and Lila
   Steve and Lila
   Jesse and Lila
NADINE: That doesn't matter
HASSAN: Goes to show
NADINE: Show what?
HASSAN: I dunno
HARPER: Shows I'm infection free
NADINE: What?
HARPER: These locks are a monument
   to how inbred this place is.
NADINE: Uptight bitch
HARPER: Sloppy seconds
NADINE: Speak for yourself
HASSAN: What?
HARPER: It's nothing.
HASSAN: Nothing?
   You two got secrets?
HARPER: No
HASSAN: Alright.
   I'll spit in her face.
   Call that even
   and you keep ya secret
HARPER: Don't

NADINE: Spit
HARPER: No
HASSAN: Not joking
HARPER: Don't
NADINE: Spit
HASSAN: Serious
HARPER: Stop.
   Don't do it
NADINE: Why not?
HASSAN: Just spill
HARPER: We can't fake this
HASSAN: Fake?
HARPER: We can't act like we're kids
   Act like we
   live in each other's pockets.
   Like this is
   anything more
   than
   a speck
   or a breath
NADINE: Sad sack
HARPER: It's true.
   I'm not coming back next year.
HASSAN: Gettin cold.
   I'm headin home.
HARPER: I can drop you two off
HASSAN: I'll walk
NADINE: We can't go yet.
HASSAN: There's nothing here
NADINE: Let's swim.
   Jump in wash the night off
HARPER: No.
   The water's still
   and low
HASSAN: Can't see
HARPER: Believe me
   I know

NADINE: How?
HARPER: The mosquitoes,
 they only lay eggs in stagnant water
NADINE: There are always mosquitoes here
HASSAN: And a shopping trolley
NADINE: Jump in with me
HARPER: No

  NADINE *climbs over the rail.*

HASSAN: Do it.
 Jump and break ya leg
HARPER: Hey?
 Come back
HASSAN: No sense
 no feeling

  And NADINE *is high above them.*

NADINE: This is living
 this is how to party.
 Climb over
HARPER: No
NADINE: The three of us
HASSAN: Join her
HARPER: It's too dark
NADINE: Let's jump in the river and swim
HARPER: Would you
 get back.
 Nadine?
NADINE: Climb over
HARPER: This is dumb
NADINE: I can hear the midges
 beating their wings
HARPER: Come back
NADINE: Jump in with me
HARPER: Do something

  HASSAN *pushes* NADINE
  and she grabs the rail

and suddenly she's frightened
and small.

NADINE: Help
HARPER: Are you serious?
NADINE: Help me back
HASSAN: Here
NADINE: You too
HARPER: Christ

And they lift her over.

NADINE: That was mean
HASSAN: Sorry
Didn't want that to—
It's was a joke
HARPER: You two can call it even.
One shirt
one scare
you're square now
HASSAN: I'm real sorry
NADINE: Okay.
HARPER: That was really—
Fuck.
That was reckless
and so stupid
you could have—
HASSAN: Pull your head in.
Nothin's changed,
you're still going
we're still here.
Think about it
HARPER: You don't think,
neither one of you
thinks past tomorrow
HASSAN: Tomorrow?
HARPER: You're locked here
you're both locked in place
HASSAN: Fuck that

Fuck tomorrow

He climbs over the rail.

HARPER: Putting on a show now?

HASSAN: Always been for show.
Now look,
look and see what I am

HARPER: A no-hoper

NADINE: Don't say that

HARPER: A nobody
A nothing.

HARPER *exits.*

The white light begins to fade.

NADINE: She's gone

HASSAN: Gone

NADINE: Come back

HASSAN: A nothing

NADINE: Makes her a bitch,
don't listen.

HASSAN: I can't hear the midges

NADINE: It's cold and dark now.
They're gone.
Walk me home?

HASSAN: Jump in and swim
like we used to
when the water was cool
and clear and clean

NADINE: Don't be an idiot.
Come back

HASSAN *starts to climb back.*

HASSAN: You owe me a shirt

NADINE *pushes him*

but he falls and she's alone in the dark.

Cassie and Saoirse

Suzannah Kennett-Lister

An old, run-down bus stop on a road that would ordinarily be busy if it wasn't so late. The light casts a grimy yellow green over the space and there is a neon glow coming from the broken bus stop advertisement— the poster it was supposed to be illuminating has been ripped out.

SAOIRSE *sits on the bus stop bench with an ornate lidded vase beside her.*

SAOIRSE: Fuck that. No way you're going to sit on the mantleplace.

Not like some useless ornament.

How fucked would that be.

Sitting there listening to Mrs Jervis every second day, just popping in to let us know that the neighbours on the other side still haven't mown their lawn and there's a dead rat smell coming from the ceiling in the hallway and had we noticed.

Not up for that.

Definitely not up for that.

CASSIE: First sign of madness!

Talking to yourself.

Ahhhhh.

Just kidding.

Right?

I do it all the fucking time.

No bother.

Sorry.

Where're you going?

SAOIRSE: Just home.

CASSIE: Bullshit.

Nice vase.

SAOIRSE: Cheers.

CASSIE: Looks real fucking expensive. It expensive?

SAOIRSE: Don't know.

CASSIE: Fuck yeah it is. Bet it is. How come you don't know?

SAOIRSE: Didn't pay for it.
CASSIE: Right cos ya stole it hey?
SAOIRSE: Not really.
CASSIE: Not really? Not fucking really. Means yeah, doesn't it?
SAOIRSE: No.
CASSIE: Given it then. Who gives a chick like you a vase like that?
SAOIRSE: Er.
CASSIE: Nah nah I'm only being a nosy fucker aren't I, hey?
      For reals though where do you get a vase like that?
      My mum would just like adore a vase like that you know?
      Just fucking adore one.
      Ya know?
      Be nice to get her one like that, hey?
      Do something nice for your mum like?
      Like get her a fuck off vase like that.
SAOIRSE: I don't think she'd want one like this.
CASSIE: How the fuck do you know what kind of vase my mum wants?
      Think you know her?
      Well you bloody don't.
      Don't tell me what my mum wants like you know. You don't.
SAOIRSE: Not saying I know what your mum—
CASSIE: Don't tell me what you're saying I know what you're saying.
      Not an idiot am I?
SAOIRSE: I don't know.
CASSIE: You don't know?
SAOIRSE: No I don't know. I don't know anything about you or your
      mum so I've got no idea if you're an idiot or not.
CASSIE: Righto. Settle down.
      Nah, my bad, hey?
      Just being nosy. Just sticking it in where it doesn't belong.
      Good thing I don't have a dick right? Be sticking that in where
   it doesn't belong hey?
      Nah nah. Joking hey. Didn't mean that.
      Rape's not funny.
      Fair enough though isn't it?
      Being nosy. You know. Curious.
      With all this shit going on everywhere, fair enough to want to
   know what it's all about.

SAOIRSE: Guess so.

CASSIE: Guess so?

You're pretty non-committal aren't ya?

Guess so don't know guess what don't know guess who who what.

Why's it got a lid?

SAOIRSE: Why has it—?

CASSIE: Got a lid?

Can't put flowers or nothing in it if its got a lid on it can ya?

SAOIRSE: It isn't for flowers.

CASSIE: Hey?

It's a vase. Vases are for flowers.

SAOIRSE: It's for my brother.

CASSIE: For your brother?

What kind of brother you got that's gonna like a vase like that?

SAOIRSE: It's not a vase.

It's an urn.

CASSIE: Oh.

Oh.

Oh fuck.

Fuck.

So that's like. That's like your—

SAOIRSE: My brother.

CASSIE: Nah don't think my mum would want that.

Some dead kid hanging out in her vase.

So he's just

Just hanging out in there?

SAOIRSE: His ashes yeah.

CASSIE: Bet he was smoking hot hey?

SAOIRSE: Um.

CASSIE: Cos they burnt him yeah? Right?

SAOIRSE:

CASSIE: Ah. Not a good one that one.

Didn't really lighten the mood like I expected.

SAOIRSE: No.

CASSIE: No. No too right.

I don't reckon I'd like that much.

SAOIRSE: What?

CASSIE: Hanging out in that.

Don't get me wrong it's real nice and everything but fuck that'd be cramped wouldn't it?

SAOIRSE: Yeah.

CASSIE: Yeah, not into small spaces.

SAOIRSE: Will didn't like them either.

CASSIE: That your brother?

SAOIRSE: Yeah.

CASSIE: Well nice to meet you William, hope you're doing alright in there buddy.

Yeah I get it. Strong silent type hey?

Did you just smile at that?

Yeah you did.

Grim sense of humour on you hey?

SAOIRSE: Guess so.

CASSIE: Guess so? Know so.

Rough trot for William though.

I reckon the best part of being dead right, is all that space you've got to explore. You know.

You get to leave behind the banality and limitations of the human form in order to explore the depth and breadth of the ever expanding, unknowable universe and he's cooped up in a fucking flower pot.

SAOIRSE: My parents want to keep him on the mantlepiece.

CASSIE: What a conversation starter.

'Oh Julie, I just love your vase.'

'Thanks Tracey. I saw it in Bed Bath N' Table and it just screamed container for the charred remains of my dead child.'

So why's he sitting here with you at a bus stop?

SAOIRSE: Because my parents wanted to keep him on the mantlepiece.

Like an ornament.

CASSIE: So you stole him?

SAOIRSE: I didn't steal him.

CASSIE: Kidnapped then.

SAOIRSE: Yeah. Kind of.

CASSIE: So what are you to going to do?

SAORISE: I don't know.

CASSIE: Well I reckon you should get him out of that ceramic prison
for a start.

SAOIRSE: What?

CASSIE: Don't you think?

I mean you said he didn't like small spaces.

SAOIRSE: No he doesn't. Never did. He got stuck in an old mine shaft
when we were kids.

That was it.

CASSIE: You know what we need to do?

SAOIRSE: We?

CASSIE: Yeah why not.

We need to go find a big fuck off space.

Like a field or a lake or something.

SAOIRSE: And like—

CASSIE: Yeah.

Tip him out.

Set him free.

Whatever.

Get the hose.

Rinse out the dregs.

Pop in some flowers—new vase for mum.

My mum.

SAOIRSE: I can't.

I want to but I can't.

Parents, you know.

He was theirs too.

CASSIE: Didn't stop you kidnapping him and taking off like Huckleberry
Finn or whatever.

So.

Now what?

SAOIRSE: I don't know.

CASSIE: Yeah you do.

Set him free, that's what.

SAOIRSE: What's it to you?

CASSIE: Nah nah, nothing.

But it's something to you.

Which is why you're sitting at a bus stop in the middle of the night with your dead brother in a pot and not at home with your rents.

    You guys close?

SAOIRSE: Fuck no.

    Will was golden child.

CASSIE: Nah not you and your rents.

    You and your bro.

SAOIRSE: Oh. Yeah.

    Yeah.

    We were close I guess.

    I'm hard to love.

    He pretended it was easy.

CASSIE: Hard to love?

    Get fucked.

    Look at you.

    You're a fucking cherub.

    I just met you and I love you.

SAOIRSE: Thanks.

CASSIE: Nothing weird or anything.

SAOIRSE: No.

CASSIE: Oi. This is where you're supposed to tell me you love me.

Bottlefeeders

Honor Webster-Mannison

SARAH *stands under a clothesline in a school uniform, fairy wings and muddy sneakers. She points to places on her body as she explains.*

SARAH: The four a.m. light makes my veins look like streets. If this vein was my street, this would be my house and this would be my next door neighbour's house and over here would be the-couple-who-I-babysit-for's house and over there would be my best friend Lucy's house, this would be my school, this would be the public pool, this is where someone else lives, and this is where blah blah lives and this is where what's-his-face lives. This is where the Collins' live. Their house is the same as mine. It's from the same catalogue. We chose it first. Right now we are here ...

She pulls up her shirt and points to her bellybutton.

... in a empty lot, a gap, a hole, a break. Last night the world was meant to end. When the world was meant to end all the council rubbish bins and dogs and leafblowers and lawns and magi mixes were gonna fall off my ears, my teeth, my chin, my fingers, my face.

SARAH *takes off her wings and hangs them on the clothesline.*

Last night I sent a boy a message that said meet me lot thirty-one under clothesline now. He came. He came in his stripy T-shirt and his braces, jeezus fucking christ braces, those braces I wanted to cut myself on those braces. They gave his mouth this kinda ... kinda carefulness. You could hear it when he said things, like when he said why'd you leave Tristan's party so early? And I said because I was bored. What I actually meant was I couldn't look at those tiny hotdogs and tomato sauce that Tristan's mum kept shoving in everyone's face. I didn't say that.

She takes off her shirt and pegs it to the line.

I take off my shirt. The boy looks at me. He looks like he's never seen a boob before. Maybe he hasn't seen a boob before. I ask if he wants to touch it. You can touch it? Maybe if he touches the boob he will be less shocked by the boob. It doesn't feel like anything. It feels like pressure. It feels like push-up bras. It feels like … I try to focus on his braces. I try to focus on the light that reflects off his braces, and the carefulness of his mouth, and the end of the world, which is imminent.

I said you can move closer if you want. You can move so close that our stomachs are touching.

She takes out her hair and threads her hair tie onto the clothesline.

He touches the underpants I borrowed from Lucy. They're purple acrylic lace.

He grinds them into me.

I'm scared of getting thrush. My mum told me you get thrush if you don't wear cotton underwear.

and he's grinding them into me.
and I'm pretty sure Lucy's had thrush
and it's contagious
and he's grinding them into me
and the acrylic lace
is itchy
like thrush.
Our stomachs are still touching.

She takes off her pants and hangs them over the clothesline.

At seven a.m. construction starts. I had my first kiss here. It's going to be residential. My first kiss was six, no five, no six, years ago and we were playing a game called either or. It's going to be a house from the same catalogue as our house. Someone picks two people and they say either or, like either Liam Davidson or Sam Pinting and you say Sam Pinting and he kisses you
and his lips feel like fish mouth
and he tastes wet and cold
and you feel like your body is yours because you can give it to someone.

Beat.

And that's how you play either or. He stops grinding the purple acrylic lace.

He will buy the house being built at seven a.m. this morning. He will go to uni and become a dental hygienist and have lots of kids who look the same and all smell like toothpaste. He won't recognise me when I walk through his house, when I forget it's his house and not an empty lot like it used to be, like it is now.

He won't recognise me because I will be different because this world will have ended and therefore I will be from a new world. A new world made out of seedlings grown out of beer bottles and baked bean cans on windowsills in houses filled with religious paraphernalia displayed in like an ironic way. I will have changed my name from Sarah to S, like S, like the letter. I will have my own purple acrylic lace underpants.

Beat.

He tells me I'm pretty. It makes me feel like I'm looking at those tiny hotdogs and tomato sauce that Tristan's mum kept shoving in everyone's face. I'm cold. He gives me the grey hoodie tied around his waist.

She takes a grey hoodie from the clothesline and puts it on.

It pools around me. It's so ugly. I tell him that I got my period so I have to go home. How can you tell? How can I tell? You can just tell when your womb lining begins to fall out of you.

And he just stares at me for a while our stomachs still touching.

Lucy told me he's got braces cos he used a pacifier all through primary school and probably still does.

I tell him this.

He leaves.

Beat.

And then it becomes the next day and the world hasn't ended. The sun rises.

The air-conditioner units
telephone poles
marriage certificates
fabric softener
lawn
house catalogues. It hasn't ended. It hasn't ended at all.

Author Biographies

Peter Beaglehole

Peter Beaglehole is an emerging playwright. His play *Strata* won the STCSA Young Playwrights Award in 2016. In 2015 he and Back Porch Theatre were awarded a Carclew Project and Development Grant to work on his play *Milk-teeth*. In 2014 he was mentored by Nicki Bloom and four emerging playwrights as part of ATYP's Fresh Ink program, and his play *May Day* was shortlisted for the Young Playwrights Award. He worked with Urban Myth Theatre Company in 2013 as an assistant tutor in their workshop program, as a dramaturg on *Pericles* and wrote a short piece of musical theatre for the Come Out Festival. He has read short fiction and personal essays with *The Hearth* and *Speakeasy*, and published micro-fiction in *Dubnium, Flinders Indaily* and *Antipodean SF*. He also researches the history of Australian drama, focusing on Dorothy Hewett's plays in production.

Ang Collins

Ang is an emerging playwright who completed her Bachelor of Arts (Languages) at the University of Sydney in 2016. She completed a playwriting intensive with Young Playwrights Inc. in New York City in 2014 and has been an active member of the Sydney University Dramatic Society as a playwright, producer and dramaturg throughout her university career. Ang is a master of the unpaid arts internship and has worked on such projects as Ros Horin's *The Baulkham Hills African Ladies Troupe* and WITS' *Festival Fatale*. She is currently studying a Masters of Fine Arts (Writing for Performance) at NIDA.

Thomas De Angelis

Thomas De Angelis is a playwright whose recent works include *Jack Killed Jack* (Sydney Fringe Festival; 2012), *The Worst Kept Secrets* (Seymour Centre; 2014) and *Unfinished Works* (Seymour Centre; 2016). After graduating from the University Of Notre Dame with a degree in Arts/Law, he attended NIDA in 2015 to study a Master of Fine Arts (Writing For Performance). In 2016, Thomas attended the ATYP National Studio at Bundanon. Thomas was the dramaturg for Jelinek's *Sportsplay* (NIDA Director's Productions; 2015) and *The Cherry Orchard* (New Theatre; 2016). He co-wrote the script for *HeySorryGottaGoBye* (Sydney Fringe Festival; 2016) and he is the co-creator and dramaturg for an original site-specific opera, *Chamber Pot Opera* (Queen Victoria Building; 2016), which will tour to Adelaide and Edinburgh in 2017.

Izzy McDonald

Izzy McDonald is an emerging theatremaker and co-artistic director of Rorschach Beast. In 2015 she graduated from the University of Western Australia, studying English and Cultural Studies. All of her artistic endeavours were completed outside of university. She has performed in: Scoopelight Theatre's regional touring shows (2013-2015); the West Australian Youth Theatre Company's *FIRE* (2013) and *Fish Out Of Water* (2014); Second Chance Theatre's *Frankenstein* (2016), and The Chaos Ensemble's *TANK* (2016). Izzy's directing debut was with her company's show *Girl in the Woo*d (2016) which won Fringe World's Best Emerging Artist and the Melbourne Fringe Ready to Tour, and was nominated for the Martin Sims Award. *Bus Boy* (2017), at the Blue Room Theatre's Summer Nights (Perth Fringe World), is Izzy's debut as a playwright She is passionate about collaboration, and making beautifully powerful stories accessible to all audiences.

Charles O'Grady

Charles O'Grady is a 22-year-old trans playwright based in Sydney. Charles has written several plays for the independent stage (*Kaleidoscope, Telescope, Before the Water Gets Cold*) and his new play *Are We Awake?* will play at the Old Fitz in March. Charles is currently working as the assistant director for Declan Greene's *The Homosexuals* at Malthouse and Griffin theatres, as well as directing high school students in a play about trans identity.

Suzannah Kennett-Lister

Suzannah Kennett-Lister is an actor, director and playwright. She trained as an actor, graduating from Adelaide College of the Arts in 2014. In 2015 she wrote and directed the original cabaret *Myriad* for the Adelaide Cabaret Festival, which has been nominated for the Adelaide Theatre Guide's Curtain Call Awards for best cabaret. She also worked as assistant director to Geordie Brookman in the State Theatre Company's production of *Betrayal,* and their collaboration with the Adelaide Symphony Orchestra, *Mendelssohn's Dream,* as well as assistant directing Someone like U's production of *Bitch Boxer* and Adelaide College of the Arts' production of *Earthquakes in London.* In 2016 she returned to Adelaide College of the Arts as an industry mentor and performed in Back Porch Theatre's debut production *Schmidt.*

Louis Klee

Louis Klee is an Australian writer who lives in Melbourne, Australia. He is the 2016 Anne Edgeworth Young Writers Fellow and a MFA candidate in writing at the VCA. His writing is forthcoming in *Meanjin* and his play *The Ink Trail* was shortlisted for the 2016 Silver Gull Award. In 2015, he graduated from the NIDA Writers' Studio

Zoe Ridgway

Zoe is in her third and final year of her Bachelor of Creative Arts at the University of Wollongong. She is passionate about dramatic writing, and upon graduation, wishes to continue expanding her work as a playwright as well as learn more about screenwriting. To date, Zoe has collaborated with Dramatic Studio, based at Wollongong's Illawarra Performing Arts Centre, who produced her short work *The Investment.* Her most recent work, *It's Actually Hockey*, explored the collective experiences of those she met when travelling India. This premiered at UOW's *Nothing to See Here* Festival 2016. She enjoys writing comedy and exploring pertinent issues to diverse and contemporary cultures.

Jordan Shea

Jordan is a graduate of the writing course at the VCA, where his major work *Trolley Boys* and its accompanying exegesis *Following the Boys* earnt him Second Class Honours under the tutelage of Raimondo Cortese. *Trolley Boys* is currently being developed in Melbourne and Sydney. Work includes: *Little Differences* (ATYP/Currency Press), *Last Drinks* (BNW Theatre), *It's been a while* (Smoking Gum) and *After Party* (shortlisted for the MTC), *CYBEC* (read as part of ASIA Topa, with dramaturgy by Chris Mead). He produced *The Stalls*, an installation piece focusing on toilet graffiti as part of the Melbourne Fringe/Arts House and has plays in development with companies around the country. Directorial credits include *Keating! The Musical* (Bryan Brown Theatre) and *The Shape of Things* (Sydney Fringe Festival/KXT) and produced *Wasn't Tomorrow Wonderful?* for Ferknerkle Productions. He completed the National Studio through ATYP, mentored by Angus Cerini, and last year worked at the National Play Festival. He dedicates this work and most of his other work to Agnes and Michael.

Lewis Treston

Lewis Treston is an Australian playwright whose work has been performed in Sydney, Brisbane and the Gold Coast. He is a graduate from QUT's Bachelor of Fine Arts (Drama) and NIDA's Postgraduate Diploma (Writing for Performance) headed by Stephen Sewell. Since completing his postgrad, Lewis' play *Reagan Kelly* (dir. Benjamin Schostakowski) has been performed at NIDA as a third-year graduation piece. He has also participated in Playwriting Australia's Dramaturgy Internship, collaborated with renowned director Jim Sharman's production company Sunday Pictures, as well as having productions and readings of his plays presented at Anywhere Theatre Festival, the Arts Centre Gold Coast, Rock Surfers Theatre Company, QUT and Short & Sweet. Other writing credits include *Pre-Drinks* and *FAT/SNOB* (dir. Danielle Carney), *Anita Elizabeth Jenson* (co-written with Nicholas K Watson), *Ghost Cafe* and *Fireworks* (co-created with Jim Sharman and Laurence Rosier Staines). In 2016 Lewis was appointed playwright in residence at ATYP.

Honor Webster-Mannison

Honor is an emerging playwright and performance artist in Brisbane. She is currently in the process of completing her undergraduate degree at the University of Queensland where she has collaborated with directors such as Sue Rider and Rob Pensalfini. Her spoken word poetry has been broadcast on Radio National and her visual art work has been exhibited at the Gallery of Modern Art. Working with a variety of mediums greatly influences Honor's performances and her interest in hybrid theatre.

Mentor Biographies

Mary Anne Butler

Mary Anne Butler is a Darwin-based playwright whose play *Broken* won the 2016 Victorian Prize for Literature, the 2016 Victorian Premier's Literary Award for Drama, the 2014 NT Literary Award for Best Script and was shortlisted for the 2014 Griffin Award. *Broken* premiered in 2015 with a sold-out season at Browns Mart Theatre, and had a Sydney season at Darlinghurst Theatre Company in August 2016. Mary Anne's play *Highway of Lost Hearts* premiered at the 2012 Darwin Festival to a sold-out season with a 2013 return season by demand, and a 2014 three-month Australia-wide tour. In 2015 it was adapted to a four-part radio series for Radio National's *RadioTonic*. Mary Anne was awarded month-long Bundanon residencies for playwriting (2016 and 2010). She is a 2014 Churchill Fellow, member of the Australian Writers' Guild Playwrights' Committee, peer advisor to the Australia Council for the Arts, and co-Artistic Director of Knock-em-Down Theatre Company (Darwin/Brisbane). She holds a Masters in Arts Education from UNE and a Master of Philosophy (Creative Writing) from the University of Queensland. Both *Broken* and *Highway of Lost Hearts* are published by Currency Press.

Angus Cerini

Angus Cerini is a playwright, performer and theatremaker. His works
have toured nationally and internationally. These include the Patrick
White Playwrights' Award-winning *Wretch* and Green Room Award-
winning *Detest (this thousand years I shall not weep)*. His production
of *Save for Crying* at La Mama received multiple Green Room Awards
including Best Independent Production and Best New Writing for
the Australian Stage. *Resplendence* as part of MTC's NEON Festival
received The Victorian Premier's Literary Award (Louis Esson Prize).
His play *The Bleeding Tree* premiered with Griffin Theatre Company
in Sydney, and has won the Griffin Award, the Sydney Theatre Award
for Best New Australian Work, the NSW Premier's Literary Award and
multiple Helpmann Awards, including Best Play.

Sue Smith

Sue Smith is a multi-award-winning screenwriter, playwright and
script editor. Her recent screen credits include: co-writer of *Saving Mr
Banks*, produced by Disney Pictures in 2013, ABC telemovie *MABO*
(screened SFF in 2012 and winner of an AWGIE and Queensland
Literary Award), ABC miniseries *Bastard Boys* (winner of AFI Award
for Best Screenplay in Television), feature film *Peaches* (nominated
AWGIE Award) and SBS miniseries *RAN*, which Sue co-wrote with
John Alsop and Alice Addison, receiving another AFI Award for Best
Screenplay in Television. Other credits include telemovies *Temptation*
and *The Road From Coorain*, and, in partnership with John Alsop,
ABC series *Bordertown* and miniseries *The Leaving of Liverpool* and
Brides of Christ, both of which won AWGIE and AFI awards.

Sue's professional theatre debut, *Strange Attractor*, received a
successful premiere at Griffin in 2009. Sue wrote the libretto for
Rembrandt's Wife, which premiered at the Victorian Opera, and won
the 2010 AWGIE award for Music Theatre. Her adaptation of Tolstoy's
The Kreutzer Sonata premiered at the STCSA to rave reviews. Her play
Kryptonite was nominated for Best Play at the 2014 Sydney Theatre
Awards. Her newest play, *Machu Picchu*, starred Lisa McCune in the
2016 program for the STC and STCSA.

Join the ATYP family.

Enhance your classroom learning with the world of ATYP. Talk to our experienced Learning Team. Visit the Wharf. Join our National Classrooms. Create something unique. Be inspired. The possibilities are limitless.

ATYP Learning connects schools with leading industry professionals. Whether your interest is in playwriting, directing, acting, technical production or promotion, ATYP Learning has something to get you started and keep you inspired.

ATYP productions, workshops, online programs and resources give you the chance to interact with all aspects of theatre. Our experienced Learning Team will help you unpack your theatrical experiences and go behind the scenes in unique and exciting ways. Join the ATYP family online or in person. We specialise in creating experiences to meet the needs of teachers and students. All of our programs are connected to State and National Curricula.

1. **ATYP PRODUCTIONS**: ATYP productions are driven by young characters and performed by our young performers. Our productions include exclusive behind-the-scenes experiences, support material, online classroom resources and interactive post show Q&A sessions. Live outside of NSW and can't make it to the Wharf? Join our National Classrooms and watch one of our live streamed performances!

2. **CREATIVE DEVELOPMENTS**: Bring a professional playwright into your classroom and be connected to a new Australian play in a totally unique way. Our Creative Developments allow your students to influence our creative artists as a play is being written and developed. Wherever you are in the country, you can be part of this unique and exciting experience.

3. **ARTIST IN RESIDENCE**: ATYP's Artist in Residence programs allow your entire school to become part of the ATYP family. One of our artists visits your school for regular workshops that build drama knowledge, integrate learning and lead to a performance. Use one of our specially-commissioned plays or work with ATYP and our professional playwrights to create the perfect script for your students.

4. **COMMISSION A PLAYWRIGHT**: ATYP also commissions new work for young Australians. Work with us, and one of our professional playwrights, to create the perfect script for your students. Embed our writing programs into your classroom.

5. **ATYP WORKSHOPS**: Visit us at the Wharf. We can come to you. Our workshops are developed as two-hour sessions or full-day intensives. All workshops cater to the needs and skill level of your students and are related to State and National Curricula. We offer workshops for primary, junior and senior students.

See a production, do a workshop. Engage with us for a term, make a date with us annually, connect the dots with a tailor-made experience. We can come to your school or community!

ATYP Learning has something for everyone. We invite you to become part of the furniture and embed ATYP into your classroom in a way that suits you and your students.

The possibilities are limitless!

Contact our friendly learning team to learn more and book your ATYP experience.

Phone: 02 9270 2400
Email: education@atyp.com.au
Website: http://www.atyp.com.au/education

More ATYP titles from Currency Press

Voices Project 2012: Tell It Like It Isn't / The One Sure Thing
A short, sharp, evocative collection of monologues written by some of Australia's leading young and established playwrights. *(Ebook only)*

The Voices Project 2013: Out of Place
A collection of seven-minute monologues with young characters that laugh, tease and tell stories to make your toes curl. What happens when people are placed just outside their comfort zone.

978-0-86819-978-8

The Voices Project 2014: Bite Me
This collection of thirteen monologues serves a mouth-watering banquet of work exploring our relationship with food. Funny, warm, irreverent and cheeky, this is a feast for the senses.

978-1-92500-507-3, or as an ebook

The Voices Project 2015: Between Us
The latest instalment of The Voices Project—the overwhelmingly successful annual program of monologues developed by ATYP, written by young people, performed by young actors around the country.

978-1-92500-535-6, or as an ebook

The Voices Project 2016: All Good Things
All good things must come to an end. Directed by one of Australia's masters of new writing, Iain Sinclair, this final season explores the theme of departures. *The Voices Project* has given a generation of young Australians monologues that speak their language.

978-1-92500-579-0, or as an ebook

The Voices Project: Encore Edition
This selection of seventeen monologues takes the reader through the themes that have been explored in The Voices Project over the years, varying from first love to food, telling the stories of Australia. By turns witty, touching and chilling, the monologues explore, deconstruct and subvert perceptions of modern Australian life.

978-1-92500-557-8, or as an ebook